2-4-6-8

How do you
Communicate?

How to make your point in just a minute

Phillip Khan-Panni

communicators

KU-557-496

BUS

CROYDON PUBLIC LIBRARIES	
Lib. H **No.** 1735 7173	
Class 658.45 KHA	
V F	**P** £6.99
Stk. 16 AUG 2001	

Published by How To Books Ltd,
3 Newtec Place, Magdalen Road,
Oxford OX4 1RE. United Kingdom.
Tel: (01865) 793806. Fax: (01865) 248780
email: info@howtobooks.co.uk
http://www.howtobooks.co.uk

All rights reserved. No part of this work may be reproduced
or stored in an information retrieval system (other than for
purposes of review) without the express permission of the publisher in writing.

© **Copyright 2001 Phillip Khan-Panni**

First edition 2001

British Library Cataloguing in Publication Data.
A catalogue record for this book is available from the British Library.

Edited by Francesca Mitchell
Cover design by Baseline Arts Ltd, Oxford

Produced for How To Books by Deer Park Productions
Typeset and design by Baseline Arts Ltd, Oxford
Printed and bound in Great Britain by Bell & Bain Ltd., Glasgow

NOTE: The material contained in this book is set out in good faith for general
guidance and no liability can be accepted for loss or expense incurred as a result
of relying in particular circumstances on statements made in this book. Laws
and regulations are complex and liable to change, and readers should check the
current position with the relevant authorities before making personal
arrangements.

Communicators is an imprint of How To Books.

Contents

This is not a long book. However, it is a little longer than you might expect for a guide to making your point in just a minute. That's because its purpose is to help you to understand how to communicate more succinctly, not only in 60 seconds, but in all situations. It is, of course, a How To book, so it contains practical advice, but it is not prescriptive. It does not simply say 'Do this!', but rather it explains why 'this' is the right thing to do.

Whenever I am training a group in presentation skills, I ask, 'Hands up if you have ever sat through a boring presentation.' Every hand goes up. I then ask, 'Hands up if you've ever given one.' Most hands go up. I'm sure you have heard people enthuse about their chosen subject in terms that mean absolutely nothing to you. And when thay have finished, you are none the wiser.

Why does that happen? Mainly, I suspect, because they have not thought through their point of view, or because they do not know why they are saying what they are saying.

If you can express yourself without excess verbiage you will always have the competitive edge. You will be interesting to listen to, you will take the high ground in group discussions, you will command the respect of your peers, clients and audiences. For that to happen you need more than technique: you need to change your own thinking.

And that's what this book aims to help you with. Succinct communication does not mean becoming monosyllabic. It means being able to get to the heart of the matter quickly, so that your listeners will want to hear more, and will give you their attention in the knowledge that it will be time well spent.

Abraham Lincoln's Gettysburg Address contains just over 260 words, and took just two minutes to deliver. Yet it is one of the most memorable speeches of all time.

Phillip Khan-Panni

To my late wife, June, who
was always my inspiration

Chapter 1

How DO you communicate?

In this Chapter:
- ◆ **why it can pay you to be succinct**
- ◆ **being persuasive**
- ◆ **you can say a lot in even 30 seconds**
- ◆ **it's amazing what people will add to what you say**
- ◆ **radio and TV ads last under a minute.**

The story is told about a young man who approached Leonard Bernstein with an idea for a new musical. Bernstein, whose impressive achievements included *West Side Story*, said, 'Write it on the back of your business card.' The young man protested, 'But I couldn't possibly fit it on the back of a business card!'.

'Then,' said Bernstein, 'it isn't ready.'

Clearly we do not always need to be as succinct as that, but it is certainly important to be able to make a point briefly. Why? Because we may have only a minute to grab the attention of someone we need to impress. And because condensing our message into a few words will help us to focus on what is really important in what we are saying.

When your chance comes, will you be ready?

Suppose you wanted a certain job, one that would fulfil your dream, a job that would express your talents and take you into the world that you craved, and reward you with the kind of earnings that you know you deserve, but which your current employer seems reluctant to give you. Suppose such a job was in the gift of a man who stopped you in the street to ask the way to the library. What would you do?

There you are, face to face with the man who could make your dream come true. He has chosen to talk to you, so you don't have to wait for an introduction.

◆ He has asked for your help, so he is receptive to you.
◆ You have sixty seconds or less to say something that will grab his attention.
◆ You've got to get him sufficiently interested to say, 'Tell me more.'
◆ It may be your only chance.

Do you tell him how great you are ... or do you tell him how great you think HE is? Are you clear about what you have to offer, and are you able to put it across in a compelling, persuasive manner? Or will you just busk it? Choose to busk it and you could blow your chances. No, you need to prepare for such an eventuality. Someone very wise said, 'It's better to be prepared for an opportunity and not have one, than to have an opportunity and not be prepared.'

The key word is FOCUS

The way to prepare is to focus on
◆ who you are
◆ what you have to offer
◆ what your message is.

You can do that in connection with your life's mission, or in connection with some specific topic. Many an aspiring professional speaker has been stumped by the simple question, 'What do you speak about?'. The true professional can tell you right away. The wannabe says, 'Oh, I can speak on anything/many things. Give me a topic and I'll prepare a speech on it.' That's what Zig Ziglar calls 'a wandering generality'.

Lack of focus can result in some very peculiar communication.

A tax helpline in Australia is reported to have had a recorded message that said, 'If you understand English, press 1. If you do not understand English, press 2.' How could anyone with an ounce of common sense record such an obviously meaningless message?

The answer lies in the focus of the person making it. When we focus on what WE want to say, going in, rather than on the OUTCOME, we risk getting it wrong. It's the cause of misunderstandings, of quarrels, of results we hadn't expected. And it gets in the way of persuasion.

You can say a lot in 30 seconds

A lot of communication is about persuasion. It can be formalised, as in a sales presentation, or it could be simply when we want others to agree with our point of view. To increase your chances of success you need to understand and apply the 2-4-6-8 process. It will guide you in preparing more effective presentations, and it will enable you to put your point across in just a minute. Have you ever wanted to tell someone to get to the point? Has it ever been said to you? Let me help you to ensure that it never happens to you again.

First, imagine that you are a public speaker and you have decided to attend my open seminar on Effective Communication. Now read this aloud, in a brisk, conversational sort of way, and take note of any pictures that come into your mind.

> I left home early to meet with you today. As I walked towards my car, I met an attractive blonde in a red dress. She touched my arm and asked, 'Where are you off to?'. I said I was giving a talk to some speakers about effective communication. I said I had half an hour to explain how to make your point in just a minute. And she laughed and said, 'Isn't that what speakers do – take half an hour to say what could be said in just a minute?'. And I wondered if you'd agree.

What did you see in your mind? Did you see the attractive blonde in the red dress? Of course you did. It's in everyone's mental 'clip art'. Now think about the size of the whole episode: didn't it feel bigger than 30 seconds' worth? Yet that's all the time it took to tell.

Now let's analyse what's in that brief narrative, and see how it provides the template for more effective communication.

1. The first sentence makes it personal to me, and establishes *common ground* with you.

2. The attractive blonde in a red dress is a strong image. It's my *hook,* to grab your attention, and to create a picture in your mind.

3. She touched my arm. She moved out of *your* imagination into *my* context, and you followed her, realising that she had some sort of familiarity with me. So you were *interested* in our conversation.

4. I stated my *theme*: effective communication in 30 seconds.

5. In order to establish a *need,* I inserted a 'criticism' – 'Isn't that what sales people do ...?'. But I made it more palatable by putting it in her words, and saying, 'She laughed ...'

6. Finally, I wanted an *outcome.* So I said, 'I wondered if you'd agree.' And that prompted you to decide for or against.

All that in 30 seconds of apparently casual conversation. So how does that translate into the 2-4-6-8 formula for more effective communication?

It's a simple example of what can be achieved in a short space of time, if you know what you are doing and understand how to press the right buttons in your listeners. This example took about 30 seconds. But you can do even more in 60 seconds. You can make your point, you can excite and interest your listeners sufficiently for them to want to hear more, and you can do all that before they have the chance to get bored.

Here's an example of a 60-second speech:

> I took a book down from the shelf and let it fall open at random. What I read made so much sense that I felt I must share it with you. It said that if you want to stand out from the crowd, the number one skill to acquire is the ability to change. And it is a skill that can be learned.
>
> It creates opportunities for progress and for beating our competitors. It is by far the most valuable skill to have, both as individuals and as a company, because our very survival depends on our ability to change to meet the needs of our market.
>
> However, we must recognise what stops us from being receptive to change, and decide what we should do about it.

The psychologist Dennis O'Grady says that there are five fears that choke our ability to change. They are:

1. fear of the unknown
2. fear of failure
3. fear of commitment
4. fear of disapproval
5. fear of success.

We need to examine how they apply to us before we can develop our strategy for progress. And that is our next priority.

Some strong reactions

I'll return to the 60-second speech later, but first let's examine the shorter speech. Whenever I have tried out the 30-second story, I have had some strong reactions. Here are a couple:

A What a woman said

One woman whom I was coaching in media interview skills said she could see me sitting in my car, talking about my plans for the day. She saw me quite clearly, with my right elbow protruding from the open window. When I gently probed for more detail, with her right hand she started pushing away some imaginary person, while telling me, 'I'm not interested in that blonde. I've no interest in her at all. Now if you'd said an attractive *brunette* ...' I said I found her reaction quite unusual, and asked why she seemed so anti the blonde (who was, after all, just imaginary), and she said, after a pause, but with a lot of passion, 'Because I'm jealous!'.

The 'clip art' image of the blonde had appeared so real in that woman's mind that she had reacted as though it had actually happened ... and as though she herself had been involved. How come?

Two reasons. The first was that the image of an attractive blonde in a red dress is a very strong one. I use it to create pictures in the minds of my listeners, to draw them into the narrative, and because real life occurs in pictures, not in words. Mental pictures give life and colour to what is being said.

However, the second reason for my client's reaction was that the image of the blonde that she created was probably based on someone she knew, or an amalgam of blondes that she knew. 'Attractive blonde in a red dress' became a kind of shorthand for blondes of her acquaintance, encapsulating not only their physical appearance but also their behaviour, their attitudes, and their relationships with my client. With the picture came the emotions, and that is why she reacted so strongly.

B What a man said

On another occasion I was training a mixed group in presentation skills, and used the same example to lead into the benefits of structure and focus. When I asked the group what they had pictured in their minds during the short narrative, every man present immediately said, 'the blonde in red'.

I then asked, 'And what did you think about her?'. They all thought I had some sort of personal relationship with her, some level of familiarity, because she had touched my arm. That was exactly the reaction I had wanted! A simple little detail like, 'She touched my arm ...' can add so much to the story because it presses a certain button in the emotions of the listeners. And there was more.

'What did you feel about that?' I asked. And one of the men said, 'I was jealous!' He wasn't jealous in the same way as my female client had been. He minded that 'his' woman, the one he had created in his own imagination, had had a relationship with me.

In the course of the story, she had moved out of his imagination and into my context, just as I had intended. I wanted to grab the group's attention and keep them interested in what was coming next, and that objective was achieved. However, one man's image became very real to him and he minded 'his woman' becoming 'my woman'. So he followed her progress from his imagination into my space, and wanted to eavesdrop on the conversation she had with me. To him it was as real as if we had met the blonde in real life, and she had chosen to be with me rather than with him. He felt the same emotions, and possibly just as strongly.

Establishing a need to listen

The next two parts of the 30-second narrative are linked.
First, because I use it in a training context, it is useful to
re-state the theme of the training, namely 'Effective
Communication'. Second, I wanted to imply a generalised
criticism of people in the occupation of those I was
addressing, partly to be provocative and partly to see if
they would agree that they had a need to improve as
communicators. I have never yet encountered resistance to
that criticism, partly because I place it in the mouth of the
blonde in red, and because she laughs when she says it.

It's a conditioning ploy, a means of preparing the listener
for the outcome I want, which is to agree or disagree.

Once I forgot to say, 'She touched my arm ...' and the
result was most interesting. Everyone present had a
different image of my conversation with the blonde in
red, and there was no suggestion of a personal
relationship between myself and her. At best she was
seen as a neighbour with whom I had a nodding
acquaintance but no familiarity.

A short cut to the heart of your listener

The blonde-in-red scenario works because it is brief, has
powerful imagery, and is structured to lead the listener
towards a planned outcome. Obviously it is limited in what
it can achieve, but the technique can enable you to open the
door to a more detailed proposition at another time.

Why is it necessary to be brief? Because most people have a very short attention span. Attention and interest tend to be given in expanding layers.

◆ **The first layer** is probably no more than 60 seconds at most, when it concerns some new idea. That means you have up to 60 seconds to make a case that will grab the attention and interest of your listeners and get them to say, 'Tell me more'. That has been well researched, and is the reason why radio and TV ads are typically 30 seconds, and seldom as long as 60 seconds.

◆ **The second layer:** Because TV and radio ads are impersonal, 30 seconds is probably the right length. Face-to-face you have more time, because your personal presence can add to the strength and appeal of your message, and because there is room for some interaction with your listeners. That's why I believe that you have up to a minute to make your point.

The most important thing to remember about making your point in just a minute is that you cannot hope to make a complete case in that time. Do not try to be comprehensive, do not attempt to include all the points or benefits that may be relevant to your proposition. Focus on a specific but limited outcome, and follow a simple structure to get you there. I'll cover structure a little later on, and take you through a number of simple sequences that will enable you to speak off the cuff on almost any topic.

Before I do that, let me comment briefly on the 60-second speech. Its purpose was to introduce the 5 obstacles to change. So I needed to give them authority, and to create a context in which they would be acceptable. My opening device, therefore, was to describe a commonplace occurrence (taking down a book from a shelf) and introduce a touch of serendipity – letting it fall open at random. The second paragraph offers the benefits of change, to condition the listener to accepting the proposition that we must overcome the 5 fears. The passage is brief, but it is well planned and directed towards an outcome.

Let me next explain what I mean by 2-4-6-8, and then let's consider the kinds of situations in which it would be helpful to make your point in just a minute.

In summary ...

- ◆ To test how ready your new idea is, try writing it on the back of a business card.
- ◆ The key word is FOCUS.
- ◆ You can say a lot in 30 seconds, if it's properly planned.
- ◆ You can say even more in just a minute.
- ◆ Use strong word pictures.
- ◆ Be ready to deliver your main messages in under one minute.
- ◆ You can create powerful reactions in your listeners.
- ◆ Aim for a specific but limited outcome.

Chapter 2

What do I Mean by 2-4-6-8?

In this Chapter:
◆ **what I mean by 2-4-6-8**
◆ **first basic principles**
◆ **facts are neutral, until they are filtered**
◆ **what you say isn't always what is received**
◆ **facts tell, feelings sell.**

2-4-6-8

2 stands for the **two basic principles** on which effective communication depends.

4 stands for the **four main situations** when you need to be able to make your point succinctly.

6 stands for **six typical obstacles** to clear communication.

8 stands for the **eight things to do** if you want to make your case successfully.

First basic principle – filter the facts

Let me ask you this: why does anyone make a speech or presentation?

Why would *you* ever make a speech or presentation? In fact, why would you have a meeting, such as a board meeting or a committee meeting? If your answer is, 'to communicate information', then why not send a memo instead?

If your purpose is simply to communicate information, my advice is to put the information on one side of a small piece of paper and mail it to your audience. That would be a much more effective and efficient means of conveying your information. The recipients would be able to read and interpret the information for themselves, and do so much faster. There would be no need to gather everyone in the same place to hear what they could read for themselves at a time that suited them best.

You could even send out the information by e-mail. Indeed, since the introduction of e-mail, there have been rather fewer meetings in some places, and a much speedier process of communication. So why do people need to hear your information in person?

Facts are neutral – until they are interpreted

There are two main reasons, and the first is that they need you to interpret the facts. You see, information on its own is neutral. It gains meaning only when it is

interpreted or placed in some context. People need to
know:

◆ what the facts mean
◆ what *you* think about them
◆ what you want *them* to think about the facts.

How tall are you? Suppose you were five foot six, you'd
be under average height in Europe and America, but in
the Himalayas you'd tower above the Gurkha policemen.
In Britain, temperatures in the eighties would be
sweltering, but in Calcutta it would be the cool of winter,
and people would be wearing extra clothes. So a height
of 66 inches is only small or tall when you know the
context, and a temperature of 80 degrees is hot or cool
according to what the norm is.

Don't assume your listener knows what to think

The same information can support both sides of an
argument. Haven't you sometimes heard someone tell
you a significant fact, only for you to wonder how you
were supposed to react to it? In your mind you ask, 'Is
that good? Is it bad?'. And you have to wait until you
get a clue. It's the same for your listeners. They may not
have the same understanding of your subject as you do,
so you may need to guide their thinking and make it
clear whether the news is good or bad.

A newspaper report may say, 'So-and-so has been sacked
as head of such-and-such a company, with a pay-off of
half a million pounds!' Ah. Should you be outraged,
because it should have been much more? Or because it's

far too much? See what I mean? Facts on their own are neutral, and when you read them on paper you cannot understand their significance unless you know the background or the circumstances that colour them.

When we deliver facts to our audiences, we should remember that they may mean much less to others than they do to us. The facts may raise your own blood pressure and point directly to some course of action, but they will usually need explaining to the audience before you can expect your passion to be shared. So you must place your personal filter over the facts you present, so that the message becomes clear.

Speaking the words is different from writing them

You may know exactly what the information means, but parts of your audience will hear it for the first time, at 150 words per minute. They cannot take in the information and interpret it correctly, all at the same time, without help from you. A lot of help.

So when you present or make a speech, do not merely hand over information in the same way as it could be presented in writing. That's a waste of time and a denial of the difference that you could make by your personal interpretation.

- ◆ Make it plain what you think of the information.
- ◆ Explain what you expect them to feel about it too.
- ◆ Help them to understand the relevance of the information.

◆ Show them where you are heading with it.
◆ Then they can decide if they would like to go along with you as well.

The same words can have different meanings to different folk

Remember, too, that other people's understanding of the terms you use may not be the same as yours. Someone I once met told me he was an engineer. Just for a joke I said, 'Oh, you drive trains?'. I explained that train drivers in America are called engineers. 'No.' he said, rather earnestly, 'I'm a civil engineer.' 'Ah,' said I, 'You're a *polite* train driver.' For a moment he looked baffled, then he laughed when he understood the point I was making, which was that labels can mean different things to different people. It would be foolish to assume that your own interpretation is shared by everyone else.

That's why it is important to filter information and explain what it means to you.

I was talking to the marketing director of a company that deals in some complex computer software. She was explaining her company's main suite of products, which involved suppliers, their customers, and the software company in a triangle of activity and responsibilities. To clarify it in my mind, I said, 'So you have three different applications.'

I meant:
(a) the customer uses the system to make buying decisions
(b) the supplier uses the system to display its range of products
(c) the software company (my client) acts as the hub through which the other two communicate with each other.

Three different purposes, so three different uses of the software system. She shook her head and replied, 'No, it's the same application.'

Only after we had circled around each other several times and repeated our respective points of view three or four times did it become evident that we were using the word 'application' in two completely different ways. I was using the word in the layman's way, meaning 'how the software can be used'. She was using the term in the computer industry's sense, in which 'application' means 'software program'.

Microsoft Word, for example, is a single application, in her sense of the word. But to me, I can use Microsoft Word as a word processor or for creating website pages, because the program has an inbuilt translator into html. It can also do mail-merge for direct mail. It can print envelopes and labels. It can let me draw shapes. So for me, the program Microsoft Word has those five or six separate applications or uses.

Jargon may make you feel 'included' but it can make your listener feel 'excluded'

It could be a lot worse. If your subject happens to be technical, there will be an overwhelming desire to use jargon. You may be tempted to justify it by claiming that your audience will be in the know, and you may even go so far as to suggest that it would be *expected* of you to employ jargon, if only to prove that you are one of the annointed brethren. Resist the urge. There is no need to show off, and there is never any justification for alienating a single member of your audience.

Here are some simple guidelines:

◆ Your task is to clarify, not to confuse.
◆ If you need to use jargon, explain and interpret it.
◆ If you are going to use initials or an acronym, spell it out the first time you use it. For example, if you want to refer to a USP, call it 'the Unique Selling Proposition or USP'.
◆ Ensure that no one will be embarrassed about not knowing jargon.
◆ Never risk losing the attention of those who need to work out what the initials or jargon might mean.

Facts tell, feelings sell

Why should you bother? Because you need to capture and retain your audience's attention and interest. For the duration of your speech, presentation or contribution to a meeting, your listeners are your prospects, and you need to convert them into customers. For that to happen, you need to establish common ground and a rapport with them. They need to see and hear what you think and feel about the information you are giving them. Only then will they realise what you expect them to think and feel about what you are telling them.

Note that I said 'what you expect them to *feel* about it.' Logical argument is not enough. Facts tell, but feelings sell. A friend was extolling the benefits of eating bananas, but nothing she said could dispel my dislike of bananas. Then she handed me a leaflet that gave the nutritional arguments. The leaflet said that bananas release sugar into the system quickly, which is useful when playing sports. Because I am a runner, that gave me a benefit I wanted, and therefore a reason to consider eating them again. The facts meant nothing until they were translated into a benefit that I wanted.

Don't leave it to them to do the translating

When we see information written down we can take our time about interpreting it. We can think about it and return to it as often as we like. We can check out whether we have correctly understood what the writer meant to say. From there we can make up our own minds about how we might put it into practice, if we so desire.

However, spoken messages are quickly gone and just as quickly forgotten – unless we make it easy for our listeners to understand the significance of our facts, and the route we want them to follow.

Remember that your audience already has a major job to do:

◆ to listen to you

◆ to understand what you are saying

◆ to decide if they agree with you or not.

It is unrealistic also to expect them to decide how to apply your message to their own lives, and to do so while they are listening to you. So make it easier for them. Do the translating for them. Tell them how they can use what you are offering.

I said earlier that facts alone are not enough, because they are neutral. We need to have a point of view. We need to deploy facts only in support of that point of view. And that presupposes that we have something to say.

That's my cue to introduce the second basic principle in the next chapter.

In summary ...

◆ **Filter the facts. That's the first basic principle.**

◆ **Facts are neutral until they are interpreted.**

◆ **Don't assume that your listener will interpret things the same way as you.**

◆ **A spoken message is not as easy to grasp as a written one.**

◆ **Make it plain what you want people to feel about what you say.**

◆ **Avoid jargon and confusing acronyms.**

◆ **Tell people how they can use what you are offering.**

Chapter 3

The Second Basic Principle: Make Change

In this Chapter:

- ◆ **the most important reason to make a speech or presentation**
- ◆ **what made Demosthenes the best orator**
- ◆ **the process of persuasion**
- ◆ **keep it relevant, and listen to the other person's point of view**
- ◆ **how you can turn the tide of a meeting**
- ◆ **when you have to be brief, you must be focused.**

Let me ask my original question again: Why do you make a speech or presentation?

The correct answer is: **To bring about change.** Change in the thinking, attitude or behaviour of your audience. If you do not intend to cause some change, why bother to make the speech or presentation?

Earlier, when I told you the story of the Australian tax helpline, I pointed out the difference between focusing on the process and focusing on the outcome. That thinking marks the difference between those who merely go to work and those who get results.

Focusing on outcome is one of the basic building blocks of effective communication.

Do you ever listen to someone speak and wonder where they are heading with what they are saying? Have you ever asked such a person, 'What's the point you are making?' We all need to know why our attention is being sought, and what we may expect to gain from listening. We have expectations of the speaker, expectations of something new. After all, if someone starts to tell you a joke you've heard before, don't you say, 'I've heard that one'?

Your starting point must therefore be the outcome you want to achieve. If you are preparing a speech or presentation ahead of time it will obviously be easier than if you are trying to make your point on the spur of the moment. But even then you will have at least a moment or two before you start speaking, to decide what you want to achieve. Sometimes, the mere act of asking yourself why you are about to say something will stop you, and save you the embarassment of saying something unsuitable or half-baked. It's far better to stay silent if you have nothing to say, than to open your mouth and remove any doubt.

The story of Demosthenes

Have you heard the story of Demosthenes? He was one of the greatest orators of all time, and lived in ancient Athens at the time when Philip of Macedon (father of Alexander the Great) was the dominant force in the region.

Demosthenes was an orphan whose guardians robbed him of his inheritance, so when he came of age he resolved to sue them. His friends urged him not to consider doing so because he had no experience of forensic law and he had a dreadful stammer. But Demosthenes was determined, so he took lessons in the law, and in how to present in the Senate, where there was a constant hubbub as groups stood about conducting their business.

He then went down to the seaside, where he practised declaiming over the roar of the waves. To overcome his stammer he filled his mouth with pebbles and practised shouting, even jogging as he did so. When eventually he went to the Senate to plead his case, he not only won but was so impressive that people came up to him and urged him to go into politics, where he came up against another great orator, Aeschines.

Aeschines was high born and well educated, with
an impressive delivery, but he tended to consider
himself rather superior. Now, here's the thing:
when Aeschines spoke, people said, 'How well he
spoke!' But when Demosthenes spoke, people
said, 'Let's march against Philip (of Macedon)!'.

I'm with Demosthenes, how about you? Which would
you rather have, applause or action?

If it's action you want, you need to be clear about what you
want to happen as a result of what you say. You then need
to understand and follow the process of persuasion. A
speech or a presentation, and even a statement of your
point of view, should be couched in persuasive terms if you
want others to adopt your thinking and take action upon it.

Let's talk about persuasion

Start by assuming that your listeners are not yet terribly
interested in your point of view or your proposition,
whatever it happens to be. Your task is therefore to
arouse their interest and take it up to and beyond the
point of acceptance, which we shall call the 'buying level'.

Step One is to attract their attention. In a newspaper
article, that's the job of the headline. In a speech or
presentation it's the job of the 'hook'. It's whatever form
you choose to say, 'Stop! This is for you!' And that's the
key: it has to be something of relevance and interest to
your listeners, and should ideally be connected to the
main benefit they will receive from listening to you.

The headline in a press advertisement says, 'Save Money!' or 'New!' or 'Last Chance!' or 'Here's something to help you live the life you want'. It may not be in those very words, but that's the sort of appeal that is contained in most headlines that work. All offer a benefit, and if that benefit is relevant to you, then you will stop and read on.

The attention-getter sharply raises interest, but usually not enough to reach the buying level, so you have a further job to do. You need to build up the interest by piling on benefits until your listeners think, 'I'd really like to have that!' or 'I entirely agree with you.'

Pile on the benefits

Think of your listeners sitting with a pair of scales in their hands – the kind with two pans. If you are selling something, they will have their pile of money in one pan. The other pan is where you must pile the benefits you are offering. As long as their pile of money weighs more than your pile of benefits there will be no sale. Only when your pile of benefits weighs more than their pile of money will they consider it a good exchange and buy what you are offering.

The same principle applies when it's not money you want, but a change in the way your listeners think and act. Then you will not be dealing with a cash cost but an inertia cost: 'I've always done things this way, why should I change?'. Or, 'I've always dealt with so-and-so, why should I deal with you?'.

Someone who wasn't listening

As I was writing this, I received a phone call from someone representing a double-glazing firm. His script went like this:

> HIM: 'I'm calling from (mumble-mumble) in Beckenham, and we are offering a free quotation ...'
> ME: 'Free quotation for what?'
> HIM: ' ... Is it Hillbrow Road you live in?'
> ME: 'I didn't catch the name of the company.'
> HIM: 'BHI. Can you confirm that you live in Hillbrow Road?'
> ME: 'What's BHI?'
> HIM: 'British Home Installations. We are offering free quotations ...'
> ME: 'Free quotation for what?'
> HIM: 'Is it Hillbrow Road you live in?'
> ME: 'Free quotation for what?'
> HIM: 'We are offering free quotations ...'
> ME: 'I asked you, free quotations for what?'
> HIM: 'For all your uPVC requirements.'
> ME: 'uPVC what?'
> HIM: 'Everything. For your doors and windows and guttering and everything. Is it Hillbrow Road you live in?'
> ME: 'I'm not interested.'

The conversation ended soon after that. But what was happening during it? He was following a script that was designed to engage me in a dialogue as early as possible, and I was refusing to play that game, because I recognised what he was attempting to do. A salesman needs to get a dialogue going because he needs to get you to agree with each of the benefits he offers. I did not want to let him get started on that process, so I interrupted his rhythm by challenging him on the identity of the company and what it offered.

Of course, I knew from the start that it was about double glazing, but I found it interesting to see how he would play his script. And the script told him to keep asking for a confirmation of my address before going any further. His next question would have been something like this: 'If we could replace your windows or doors for no/little cost, how many would you replace?' It's a hypothetical question, but it keeps the dialogue flowing. Although I did not respond as I was supposed to, I approved of the thinking behind the script. My main reservation was with the caller's unwillingness to answer MY questions. The result was a confrontation rather than a dialogue, because he was not interested in my point of view, only his own.

However, when you are trying to make your point in just a minute, that whole process has to be condensed. You have only seconds to seize the attention of your listeners, and not much longer to whet their appetite for your real message.

The change you can bring about in just a minute is just as important as when you make a speech or presentation, but it has to be different. Mostly it will be a change in their attitude to you, going from indifference to a willingness to give you a fuller hearing.

What will bring about such a change?

Focus on what will achieve your outcome

It could be something startling or unexpected, but usually it will be some form of self-interest. As you know, everyone's favourite radio station is WII FM – What's In It For Me? So if you start with a powerful attention-getter, then appeal to self interest, you have a strong chance of achieving your outcome. And that's where we came in.

If you have only a minute to make your point, you must have a very clear idea as to the outcome you want. Think again about the example of a chance meeting with the one person who could make your dream come true. What will you say? What is it that you want that person to do for you? If you don't know, or cannot say it, you've probably blown your chances forever.

Take that same thinking into a business meeting. The others sitting around the table will probably talk around the subject until they arrive at a position they feel comfortable with, and the meeting will drag on longer than necessary. Does that sound familiar? Then one person can turn the whole discussion around simply by making a succinct, well-directed contribution that points the others towards a specific course of action. That person could be you. Not only will you gain several brownie points, but you will be perceived as someone to follow.

In summary ...

♦ Aim to bring about some change.

♦ Start with your end in mind.

♦ What outcome do you want?

♦ Be like Demosthenes: get action rather than applause.

♦ Pile on relevant benefits.

♦ Pay attention to your listener's point of view.

♦ Stay focused, be succinct, call for specific action.

Chapter 4

Don't Be Boring

In this Chapter
- ◆ **the four situations when brevity and directness count**
- ◆ **what's the point you are making?**
- ◆ **the difference a structure makes**
- ◆ **three common weaknesses**
- ◆ **the danger of self-indulgence when you rise to speak**
- ◆ **understanding how people listen**
- ◆ **never cross the boredom threshhold.**

There are four situations in which it is important, or even essential, to be succinct. Two are informal, two are formal. The informal situations are:
1. in your private life
2. at work, among close colleagues, or within your own department.

The two formal situations are:
3. at work, for example when presenting to the Board or to other departments
4. when presenting or speaking to clients or prospects.

Get to the point

Have you ever said to a friend or acquaintance, 'What's the point you are making?' or 'Can you get to the point?' Has it ever been said to you? And have you ever sat through a boring presentation? If your answer to any of those questions is yes, you know why it is important to be able to put your point across as economically and directly as possible.

No-one has the right to be boring. And anyway, if you have something to say, why not try to make it as compelling as you can? I recently attended a meeting that was addressed by three distinguished speakers, one after another. They were all recognised experts in their fields, with high profiles and books to their names. They had the kind of knowledge and experience that I wanted to hear and take away.

Common weakness 1: the absence of structure

I made notes as they spoke.
- The first speaker was deliberately contentious, in order to spark debate, but he had lots of good things to say.
- The second speaker was not as well known, but he had a well-defined structure, and a point of view that he developed through the use of analogy. He was easy to follow.
- The third speaker, however, spoke for twice as long as the other two. There was **no discernible structure** and very little substance.

She would ask rhetorical questions like 'What is the price of success?' and raise my hopes of something interesting to follow. Instead, she then opened brackets and gave us a torrent of words about some rather irrelevant background events. The stuff in brackets took several minutes, so that we'd forgotten the main point by the time she returned to it. That was the pattern of her speech: one boring bit of gossip after another, with no obvious point to any of them. The gossip flooded over us, leaving us bewildered and unable to take notes. I gave up and put my pen away. So did everyone else.

This caused her to add even more energy to the irrelevant torrent of words, until we felt we were drowning, desperate for relief. Lasting 40 minutes in all, the speech wrecked the evening, ending it in an anti-climax and taking away from the two excellent presentations that had preceded hers.

Common weakness 2: self indulgence

On another occasion, I attended a dinner at my sports club, which was to be addressed by a sports celebrity. The club steward, whom I shall call Ken, had arranged the occasion and managed the catering. Ken acted as host, and took it upon himself to introduce the guest of honour. He spoke for three quarters of an hour. He reminisced. He dropped names. He talked of his own (long-gone) sporting career. He told us of how he had followed the guest of honour's sporting career. He gave us an extended history of our club. He added stories and a weak joke or three. He burbled, he bored, he brought us to our knees. For 45 interminable minutes. The hands on the clubhouse clock seemed to crawl along like rush-hour traffic on the M25.

Finally, he handed over to the guest of honour who by this time must have been feeling like a wet rag. What is certain is that he wasn't facing a well warmed up audience, but one that was praying for silence, or an early death, or at least the loyal toast so that they could relax and perhaps light up a cigar. On the positive side, the speaker could have been indifferent (in fact he was brilliant) and we'd have loved him, because he was welcome relief from the torture of the man who had introduced him.

What is it about people like Ken and the speaker in the previous example that causes them to inflict such pain upon their audiences? There may be several explanations, but two in particular are worth noting. The first is that they are self-centred. They are insensitive to the needs and reactions of their listeners because they are focused on what *they* want to say, in a self-indulgent way. The second is that they lack the discipline to stand up, speak up and shut up.

Common weakness 3: capping stories

A more common example of this species is the person who caps your stories. You tell of an incident that happened to you on Eurostar when you went to Paris last week and they will immediately say, 'I had an even more incredible experience the first time I travelled by Eurostar.' Sound familiar?

Let me now confess that I was once a story capper myself. In my mind I thought I was adding value to the other person's story, moving the narrative along with my own contribution. It took a friend with sufficient nerve to tell me the truth when I wondered why people would move away once I had joined the conversation. 'It must be because of the way you cap their stories,' she said. I had no idea I'd been giving offence. Similarly, when I have told others that they were capping stories, like me they had thought they'd simply been adding to the stories of others.

We don't always know when we go on too long

Capping stories is not the main point I want to address in this chapter. However, it is a symptom of the kind of attitude and insensitivity that can make a person boring. We don't always realise we are being boring or giving offence. In our personal circles we may not be told, because people are usually too polite to tell us we talk too much or too selfishly.

Try this. Carry a stop watch and time how long certain people speak without interruption. In conversation, if you speak for more than three minutes without allowing someone else to say something, you are boring. Do you think three minutes is a long time? It certainly is, and it can make you feel you are being lectured at. Yet it's amazing how many people hog the conversation in that way, and often for stretches that far exceed a mere three minutes.

In conversation, anyone who talks without interruption for more than three minutes is giving a speech and trying the patience of his or her listeners. Conversations are two-way streets, and those who forget that are boring.

How people listen

Let's take a moment now to consider what happens in the minds of those who are listening to you.

The average person thinks at about 500 words a minute. You probably speak at an average of 150 words a minute.

That leaves a surplus capacity in their minds of 350 words a minute – more than double that required to follow what you are saying. As you speak, you will obviously want them to stay with you on **Track 150**. However, every time you say something that they do not understand, or do not agree with, or which they find boring, their minds will drift into **Track 350**.

500 wpm

150 wpm	350 wpm
You need to keep your audience on Track 150.	Here's where people deal with other thoughts and side issues.
	You drive them here if you say something they don't immediately understand.

Keep in mind that no-one will stay concentrated on your words 100 per cent of the time, in any case. Inevitably, thoughts will intrude. It could be about their breakfast, their train journey, the bills they have to pay, the wonderful time they had last night ... anything at all. That's just natural, and it happens to all of us. We can hold on to those stray thoughts or we can let them go. But it means that while we have those thoughts in our minds we are not listening.

If you say or do anything that causes your listeners to drift into Track 350, you have less chance of persuading them to your point of view. And if you go on rather long, they are certain to take refuge in Track 350, because it's less uncomfortable there, and they don't have to endorse what you are saying.

In a productive dialogue, there is an exchange of views. While you are speaking, your listener adopts one of six typical stances:

1. agreeing with you and having his or her own point of view confirmed
2. endorsing your point of view by acquiescing through silence
3. listening to learn something new
4. trying to understand, and wanting to clarify or challenge points of detail
5. disagreeing and waiting for a chance to say so.

The dialogue is productive because your listener's attention is engaged and there is the likelihood of some contribution to the conversation. The problem arises when you go on talking for too long, and without allowing natural gaps for the other person to respond without being rude. That leads to stance number 6: the switch off. If you don't allow the other person to come in, it stops being a dialogue and becomes a monologue. And that's boring. So the other person stops listening and just waits for your lips to stop moving.

There are, of course, other ways in which a person can be boring, and one of the purposes of this book is to help you avoid those traps.

How to avoid being a bore

The main thing is to have something to say, and to say very little if you don't have something to say. An old saying goes, 'Blessed is the man who, having nothing to say, refrains from giving wordy evidence of the fact.'

A bore is someone who:
♦ makes pronouncements on every subject that arises
♦ goes one better than everyone else
♦ talks too long
♦ tells the same stories repeatedly
♦ is in love with the sound of his own voice
♦ pins you in a corner at parties
♦ monopolises the conversation or any individual.

Worst of all, a bore is someone who has no interest in what anyone else has to say. He or she is the kind of person whose eyes glaze over when you try to share in the conversation, as much as to say, 'Why aren't you simply listening to the most interesting person in the world – ME?'

The way to avoid being such a person is to be interested in what the other person is saying, to make your own point sparingly and, when appropriate, to get directly to the point. You can always elaborate if your listener wants you to, but never impose the elaboration on your listener.

In summary ...

◆ **Be succinct in two informal and two formal situations.**

◆ **Never let anyone tell you to 'get to the point'.**

◆ **Follow a structure and avoid rambling.**

◆ **When you're introducing someone, don't make a speech.**

◆ **People avoid those who cap their stories.**

◆ **Remember to keep your listeners on Track 150.**

◆ **Remember WIIFM and you won't be boring.**

◆ **Make your point succinctly then let others speak ... and LISTEN.**

Chapter 5

How Easily Do You Communicate?

In this Chapter:

◆ **common problems of interpretation**

◆ **the serious consequences of getting it wrong**

◆ **cultural differences can bring misunderstanding**

◆ **do you say it right?**

◆ **when they stop listening to what you're saying**

◆ **the real test of your communication skills**

◆ **how to get others ready to accept what you say.**

You may think you are clear in your own mind about what you want to say, but what you say may not be what is received. For example, I was planning a training programme with a colleague one day and we were discussing a session on impromptu speaking. I wanted to do it differently from the usual formula of calling up each person in turn and asking them to speak for two minutes, without prior warning, on a subject of our choosing.

In my mind I envisaged an accident scene in which each person present would have something quite different to say about what actually happened. So I said, 'Let's decide on a theme and then interview each person for two minutes.'

My colleague, thought for a moment, then said, 'Oh, so they'll all be applying for the same job?'

''Scuse me? What's this about a job?'

'You said they are to be interviewed. Are they supposed to be applying for a job? The same job?'

Same word, different meanings

Now, I had been thinking about a media-style interview. Vox pop. Microphone under the chin, tell us what happened, who was to blame, that sort of thing. My colleague, on the other hand, was due to sit on a recruitment panel the following week, so for her the word 'interview' meant 'job interview'. Her use of the word was determined by her current experience. The context was provided by the thing that was occupying her mind at the time.

More recently I sat in on a seminar on copywriting. The presenter, Stuart Goldsmith, who happens to be a staggeringly successful copywriter, but possibly too influenced by Americanisms, declared that he was going to give us some examples of what he called 'killer openings' to direct-mail letters. He was well into his third example before one member of the audience interrupted to say, 'Actually, I think these examples are really quite good, and I'm having difficulty understanding why you think they are not.'

Stuart laughed and said, 'They *are* good. In fact, I think they are *very* good. That's why I call them "killer openings".' He used the term 'killer' to mean 'very good'. His listener understood the term 'killer openings' to mean 'openings that kill the sale'.

Such misunderstandings occur so frequently that we laugh them off or simply correct them and move on. They retreat into insignificance so that it's hard to recall specific examples, even though we might all agree that they do happen all the time. The trouble is, they could (and do) occur with serious or potentially serious consequences.

The consequences can be serious

A psychotherapist friend of mine was asked to go out to the Middle East to help a family with a 'special needs' problem. The case proved particularly difficult, and the family member with the problem, whom I shall call Abdul, was especially resistant to my friend's help. While discussing the situation with Abdul's mother, the psychotherapist laid out the available options, one of which was to withdraw temporarily, and see how it affected Abdul.

What she actually said was, 'I could go back to England.'

Within 24 hours, Abdul's mother had booked my friend a flight back to England, expressing regret that she was giving up on the case. Abdul's mother had interpreted 'I could go back to England' as being a declaration of intent, whereas it had been merely a statement of one possible course of action.

There were, of course, significant consequences that flowed from that simple linguistic misunderstanding. Not only was the therapy halted at a critical moment, but the relationship between client and therapist was spoiled. It turned out to be more than just a linguistic misunderstanding, but a cultural one as well, because the client was male and Arab, while the therapist was female and European. In the client's world, females (other than mothers) are not expected to take the initiative in ending a dialogue.

Cultural influences can make a big difference to the way in which words, phrases and even inflections are interpreted. Those cultural differences occur not only between nations but also between social classes and between people from different parts of the country. We need to be aware of them and take account of them if we are to communicate effectively. It's even more important if we have little time to make our point.

It could be the way that you say it

Consider this simple example:

'I was born in London.'

How many pieces of information do you think are included in that short sentence? One? Two? Try reading it aloud and think about what you have said. (And, for the sake of the exercise, let's assume that you really were born in London.)

Now let me ask you five questions. I'd like you to answer every question using the same five words – all five of them each time.

1. Who was born in London?
2. You weren't really born in London, were you?
3. Have you ever been to London?
4. Were you born anywhere near London?
5. Where were you born?

If you were careful your answers should have been:

1. *I* was born in London.
2. I *was* born in London.
3. I was *born* in London.
4. I was born *in* London.
5. I was born in *London.*

Five quite different pieces of information contained in that short, five-word sentence. Just shifting the emphasis altered the meaning in some significant way.

Cross-cultural sensitivities

Now consider this. Suppose you were speaking to someone of West Indian or Indian appearance, and you asked, 'Where were you born?' What would you think if the answer was, 'I *was* born in London!' Wouldn't you think the answer was a bit defensive?

You might even say, 'Hang on, I wasn't challenging you, or doubting that you were born in England.' In no time at all you could then find yourself in a heated situation, and all because the wrong syllable had been accented. There could be a wealth of meaning behind the wrong response. (I once tried the exercise with a large group of salesmen. I went along the front row and asked five different people the five questions, one each. The final question, 'Where were you born?' was addressed to someone of obvious foreign origin. With a thick accent he replied, 'I was born in Sri Lanka.'

Everyone in the place laughed, except him. He hadn't understood the exercise and he didn't understand why the others laughed. It was a lesson for me, and I've been more careful since then to ensure that people do understand what I'm asking them to do, and why.

Try describing a colour to a blind person

Now try this simple exercise with a friend. Get him or her to sit with closed eyes while you describe some everyday object such as a pen, an ashtray, or a television set. You have to assume that your friend has been blind since birth and has never before encountered the object you are describing. Your friend must challenge you on anything you say that he or she cannot be expected to understand, as someone who has never been able to see.

Now get your friend to draw what you described, based entirely on your description. A good idea would be to switch on a tape recorder as you describe the object, and rely on the recording alone to assist your friend in completing the drawing. No further explanations from you.

Now put your heads together and list the main obstacles to clear and effective communication. It should have been an easy exercise, but I think you'll find that it's actually rather hard to re-create in the other person's mind the image you started with.

When I tried this exercise with a group of people, some of the descriptions of a pen included these statements:

It's about six inches long. (What's an inch?)
It has a barrel containing ink. (What's ink?)
It has a nib ... (What's a nib?)
... that's gold in colour. (Gold? Colour?)
... that leaves a mark. (Blind people cannot understand leaving a mark.)
You can write with it on paper. (Do blind people 'write'?)
It has a clip. (Another assumption.)

What you say isn't always what is received

Here's a different drawing exercise. This time you will be giving instructions to someone else, so that they can reproduce the drawing below.

Sit back to back so that you cannot make eye contact.

You should not be able to see what the other person is drawing, and he or she must not be able to see the original that you are describing. There are two levels of difficulty: one, no questions are allowed (i.e. no feedback) and two, with questions allowed for clarification of instructions, nothing else.

Here are the rules you should read out to the other person:

> I am going to describe to you a simple figure, to enable you to reproduce it as closely as possible to the original that I am holding. The figure is made up entirely of geometrical shapes, i.e. squares, rectangles, triangles and circles. I shall not be telling you if it resembles anything you know, such as a house, a car, or an implement of any sort. I shall simply tell you what shapes to draw.

1. You are not allowed to ask questions.
or
2. You are allowed to ask questions, but only to clarify the instructions.

Set a time limit of, three to five minutes, no longer, otherwise it becomes laboured. At the end of the period, see how closely the other person's drawing matches the original. If more than one other person played the game, see how similar the drawings are to one another's. Rarely will you find any two drawings the same.

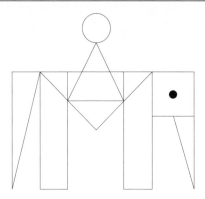

What problems did you encounter?

Let's now consider the problems that you may have encountered in doing those exercises. First of all, did you find it easy to describe the everyday object? And what about the last exercise? Was it easy to convey the assortment of geometrical shapes?

I have conducted both exercises with several groups and never once seen two identical drawings reproduced. Nor have I heard a pen described sufficiently well to enable a blind person to understand what it was supposed to be or do.

Both exercises are useful indicators of how difficult it is to put across a seemingly simple idea. In our day-to-day exchanges we probably assume that what we say is clearly understood, and that the idea we start with is accurately received by others. Often we use a kind of verbal shorthand that presumes a common vocabulary between ourselves and others. When you give instructions, for example, are there gaps that others have to fill by guessing at what you meant?

Consider this next passage.

Road signs: What do you think of them?

Think about your experience on the roads, when you drive to some unfamiliar destination. You follow the signs until, at some crucial moment, the signs run out. You reach a T-junction and there's no indication as to which way you should go. Or there are signs to local places that mean nothing to a stranger in those parts.

The first time I drove to Egham in Surrey I found myself joining the A308 at a roundabout that pointed one way towards Windsor and the other way towards Kingston. No mention of Egham, so I had to guess. And you can drive forever up and down the A3 if you don't know whether Richmond is above Twickenham or the other way around.

Don't you often wish you could get hold of the persons responsible for road signs and force them to drive around following the signs alone, so that they get hopelessly lost? And don't you wonder if they ever go out and see for themselves if their signs are adequate, accurate and visible at speed?

We have things in common, don't we?

All right, now let me explain what I've just been doing.

By citing some common experiences, I have been encouraging you to nod your head in agreement, so that we have similar terms of reference and some common ground. Once that happens, I can start introducing new ideas or information. It's much harder to persuade you to my point of view until I do that. Think about two dogs meeting each other in the street. What's the first thing they do? That's right, they sniff each other. That sniffing period is vital to removing suspicion and establishing whether they are friends or foes. It's equally important between humans.

This book is about getting your point across quickly and effectively. You therefore need to be aware of the key dynamics involved in direct communication:
◆ getting under the other person's guard
◆ gaining acceptance
◆ presenting your new thinking from a stance that is alongside, not opposite, him or her.

As the song puts it, 'Let me take you by the hand and lead you through the streets of London / I'll show you something to make you change your mind.'

The key words there are 'take you by the hand', 'lead you', 'show you' and 'change your mind'. Think back to the 30-second story in Chapter 1 about the attractive blonde in a red dress. My opening sentence was, 'I left home really early to be with you today.' That establishes some **commonality**: it says I made some effort on your behalf, I set out with you in mind, I was thinking of you, you are important to me. How do you react to someone who thinks of you, does something for you, tells you that you are important? Aren't you more receptive to such a person?

That is the starting position. It establishes rapport and empathy. However, there are still a number of possible obstacles in the way of clear communication, and we shall consider them in the next chapter.

In summary ...

- ◆ The same words can mean different things to different people.
- ◆ Check that you and your listeners are on the same wavelength.
- ◆ Practise matching your emphasis to the meaning you intend.
- ◆ Be alert to cross-cultural differences and sensitivities.
- ◆ Develop the ability to describe things clearly to a blind person.
- ◆ Establish commonality to create rapport and empathy.

Six Common Obstacles to Clear Communication

In this Chapter:

◆ **common problems of interpretation**
◆ **terms of reference**
◆ **how others want you to communicate**
◆ **cross-cultural considerations**
◆ **6 typical obstacles that we erect ourselves.**

I'm going to consider some typical obstacles to clear communication. There could be many likely candidates, but we'll limit ourselves to just six. First, let's go back to the drawing exercise. What were the difficulties?

Every time I conduct this exercise with a group, I see looks of puzzlement growing on their faces, and one by one they put down their pens and give up. When I ask, 'Who's having problems?' every hand shoots up.

Why do they give up? Because it becomes increasingly difficult to visualise what is being described, because words alone are often not enough.

◆ We need gestures.
◆ We need eye contact.
◆ We need interaction.

This last involves a great deal of body language shorthand, with confirmation and correction guiding our moves and allowing us to move as fast as we choose. We need feedback to let us know how we are doing and to guide us in modifying our communication in order to get a better result. The absence of eye contact forces us to rely entirely on the words being used, and that inevitably raises the problem of interpretation, while slowing down the process of communication as well.

True communication is a two-way process. It seldom works well if we simply transmit without establishing if it is being properly received, or whether our listeners can properly understand what they are receiving.

Do you give enough detail?

Incomplete

One of the most common complaints I have heard in such an exercise is that the information given was incomplete. When it involves drawing geometric shapes, people like full instructions, including dimensions, angles and locations. Think back to your schooldays, specifically to your maths lessons when you were first being taught geometry. I know the memory is probably painful but do try.

Terms of reference

What's the first thing your teacher did after drawing a triangle or a rectangle on the blackboard? Wasn't it to letter each corner, A, B, C, and so on? Why was that necessary? Obviously because it made it easier to give and understand instructions about any of the angles or sides involved in the problem under consideration. Did you consider lettering the corners of the diagram when you described the drawing? There was no reason not to do so.

If your focus is on helping someone else to understand what you are saying, so that they can do something with it, surely it's right to add any elements that will help that result to come about. Consider this example:

I'm surprised I ever got there

> I was due to make a presentation at a one-day event at a hotel about 150 miles from where I live. I asked the hotel to send me directions, as it was located in a semi-rural setting. The directions they sent me were for approaches from all over the country, and I was expected to leap from the end of the paragraph headed 'From the South' to the middle of the paragraph headed 'From the South West'. That didn't matter quite so much as two other things.
>
> The first was the critical section that dealt with where I should go after exiting the motorway. It said, 'Go straight across the 1st roundabout, following the road towards Birmingham. Go straight across at a number of traffic lights and straight across at the next roundabout. There are several more traffic lights, continue straight across these, remaining on the same road. Take the exit for the City Centre ...'

How many traffic lights? And since that stretch covered some two miles, I was in a constant state of anxiety that I may have overshot the designated exit. At the very least they could have included some landmarks – terms of reference – so that I woud feel reassured that I was still on track.

The second problem occurred over the final part of the directions which read, 'Straight across the next roundabout and at the T-junction at the top of the road turn right and the hotel is 100 yards on the left.' I crossed the roundabout and, some distance away, came to another roundabout, at the ring road. No T-junction. So I retraced my steps, then rang the hotel. They said to return to that second roundabout, then take the first exit left (not right, as on the original directions) and exit the ring road at Junction 9.

Eventually I found the hotel, but it was about three miles and several degrees of blood pressure distant from the 'exit for the City Centre' mentioned above, which I had assumed to be perhaps about half a mile from my destination.

What would have helped? More detail and some indication of the distance between key points along the way.

The first obstacle to overcome

Incompleteness is the first obstacle to clear communication. It matters even more when you have to be brief. When you have little time to make your point, every word must count, and no important detail can be left out. Imagine meeting someone really interesting and inviting them to your home, giving them directions to get there, but omitting the name of the road you live in, or your house number in the road. Wouldn't that present your new friends with a challenge?!

Giving directions can be difficult. But following them can be even harder. Even if the information is clear inside your own head, it needs to be precise, complete, and told with a proper understanding of your listener's point of view. Some people have a knack for getting such things right. My son is one of them, but he's an airline pilot, so I suppose he has well-developed navigation skills. The very same evening as I had trouble finding the conference hotel, I rang my son at his new house in Nottingham. He gave me rapid-fire directions, which I managed to scribble on a piece of paper. I followed them exactly and arrived at his house without any problem.

What was different? He understood what he would need to know, in my position, so he told me everything I needed and nothing that I did not need.

People's expectations can get in the way

Let's return to the drawing exercise. Here are some of the comments I have heard from those who had difficulty following the directions:

'You should have said where the picture was to be placed on the page.'
'You didn't say the page had to be landscape.'
'It would have helped if you'd called that an iscosceles triangle.'
'I would have started with the central triangle ...'
'I hate geometry, so my mind closed as soon as you started.'
'We needed some sense of scale. You should have told us how big the overall picture was going to be.'
'Why didn't you give us the dimensions of each line?'

'You should', 'I would' – these are the expressions of personal expectations not being met. Some people prefer to have information presented in a particular way and they resist any different approach. It means they aren't really listening and will be among the first to put down their pens and fold their arms across their chests. The fault, they will say, lies with the person giving the directions, who should realise that there is a better way. My way.

Our built-in expectations can be obstacles to understanding. There are, of course, certain conditions that make it impossible or very difficult to understand. Blindness, deafness and other physical disabilities are examples of unavoidable problems. In addition, there are cultural considerations. Some nations, such as the Germans and the Finns, tend to be very direct in their speech, and that can lead them to be puzzled by the less direct style of some other nations.

Fact or feeling? The Germans, in particular, are impatient with communications that are not packed with fact and substance. They tend to disbelieve extemporaneous presentations and would resist emotional appeals, unlike the Italians and Spanish, who are much more 'touchy-feely'. More than that, the Latins tend not to listen very closely, because they want you to confirm what they already believe or know. Think what happens when an Italian family meets another family in the street. Both sides start shouting the moment they catch sight of each other, and they carry on talking over one another. They are therefore unlikely to listen in respectful silence, hoping to learn something new from you. For that you need to catch them unawares.

Cross-cultural considerations. A colleague of mine who specialises in cross cultural training told me of the first time she addressed an audience of Finnish business people. She left time at the end for questions, but not one hand was raised. To help her along, the event organiser asked a couple of questions, and the whole session ended rather limply. Soon afterwards she addressed another similar group, and once again there were no questions. In some exasperation she asked them why, and one of them said, 'You must remember that we are Finnish. We believe that if it was important enough to be said, you would have included it in your talk. If you did not include it in your talk, it wasn't important enough to say. So why should we ask questions to get you to say what you had already decided to leave out of your talk?'

So how should you deal with the expectations of others?

Six typical obstacles to clear communication

Here are some of the obstacles that might become apparent:

◆ **Incompleteness:** did you give a full description?
◆ **Beliefs:** our lifelong conditioning (like blindness) makes us prone to particular interpretations of words or ideas.
◆ **Unclear:** we know what we want to say, but is that what the other person actually receives?
◆ **Irrelevant:** In the exercise, as in day-to-day communications, do we clutter the message with irrelevant detail?
◆ **Language:** the same word can mean totally different things to different people.
◆ **Terms of reference:** If you don't establish common ground, it will be so much harder to create a picture in the other person's mind. If you are describing a pen to a blind person, use terms that mean something to that person.

The acronym for those six obstacles is **I BUILT**. Because most of those obstacles are erected by ourselves.

In summary ...

◆ What you say isn't always what others hear.
◆ When you give directions, do you
  - understand what the other person needs to hear?
  - include enough detail?
  - use appropriate terms of reference?
  - avoid confusing repetition?
◆ Establish early on how others want you to communicate.
◆ Remember that different nations have different expectations.
◆ I BUILT represents six obstacles that we erect ourselves.

Chapter 7

Words that Work

In this Chapter:

- **understanding the power of language**
- **the difference between the written word and the spoken word**
- **the importance of rhythm in speeches**
- **words that work the imagination**
- **Shakespeare, the master communicator**
- **when directness pays.**

The right choice of words will make a big difference to the vividness of your communication. It will also require fewer words to take your listeners to the top of the mountain. The kind of word choice I have in mind is direct, emotive and action-based. Or it could be the kind of words that tap into the mental 'clip art' of your listeners, producing strong, clear images, as in the 30-second narrative I used in Chapter 2, when I talked about encountering an attractive blonde in a red dress.

This chapter interrupts the flow of 'How To' guidance, to dwell a little on language. I call the chapter 'Words That Work' because there are words that can add value and bring power to your message. They should not be chosen in a mechanical way, but rather through a feel for the beauty of language. Sometimes it will be individual words that make the difference, at other times it will be the way we structure what we say, so as to awaken the emotions of our listeners and take them from the first nod of agreement to full-blooded enthusiasm for action.

I hope to lead you to an appreciation of the power and the subtleties of language, and how to use it for more effective speeches. Starting with something very simple, remember this example from Chapter 5:

'I was born in London'

You can say it five different ways, just by shifting the emphasis to a different word. Each time the meaning changes, and if you emphasise the wrong word, even by a fraction, your listener can pick up a meaning you did not intend. That tells us that:

1. Even simple words can convey quite different meanings.
2. The speaker can put across wrong message.
3. The listener can get it wrong.

Using the right words in the right way will get your message across effectively, help you to bring about the change you want, overcome resistance, and take your speaking skills to a higher level.

Spoken language versus written

Everyone knows that the way we speak differs from the way we write, but it isn't always easy to use the right vocabulary in each case. Even so-called experts can get it spectacularly wrong. Here's an example I found in a book called *The Handbook of Communication Skills*, which states in the blurb: 'effective communication is arguably the single most important feature of business success.' Then on page104 it states:

> 'The implications of identifying underperformance and having individual remedies applied has undertones which could conceivably be interpreted as sinister or threatening to staff.'

What does it mean? Perhaps it could have been expressed like this:

> 'When considering why staff underperform, it's dangerous to propose a different remedy for each person, because that will appear to separate each one from the group. All will then feel threatened.'

The second version is not only simpler and more direct, it also answers the vital 'so what?' question. Why 'sinister and threatening'? Because it makes each person feel too closely observed, and separated out from the group.

How the spoken word differs from the written word

The three main differences between written and spoken language are:

1. vocabulary
2. sentence length and structure
3. oratorical devices such as rhythm and repetition.

1. Vocabulary

Words have a number of functions beyond merely conveying their dictionary meanings. These could be:

◆ acting as labels that create mental images in listeners' minds
◆ conveying shades of meaning (and therefore can be misunderstood)
◆ stirring powerful emotions through preconceptions
◆ placing the speaker in a pigeon-hole, especially in Britain
◆ including or excluding the listener: slang, jargon, shibboleths.

Words can mean different things according to context. A teacher asked a class if the word 'love' is a noun or a verb. One boy wrote, 'On Friday and Saturday nights it's a verb. The rest of the week it's a noun.'

◆ Use words of everyday speech. Complex words cause a pause for thought, and a break in communication.

- Use words that convey commitment and passion.
- Avoid words whose opposites sound similar if spoken quickly,
  e.g. inconsiderate, insubstantial, unconcerned.
- Use positive, stand-alone versions, such as selfish rather than inconsiderate, casual or aloof rather than unconcerned, flimsy rather than insubstantial.
- Avoid words that cause listeners to stop and think, e.g. disingenuous, protagonist.

2. Sentence length and structure

- In speeches, break up the sentences into bite-sized pieces.
- Get to the point early – avoid subordinate clauses.
- Use occasional short sentences for dramatic effect and emphasis.
- Use repetition for rhythm, dramatic effect and to build up to a climax.

3. Rhythm and repetition in famous speeches

'For courage, not complacency, is our need today. Leadership, not salesmanship. And the only valid test of leadership is the ability to lead, and lead vigorously.'

'Let us never negotiate out of fear, but let us never fear to negotiate.'

'Ask not what your country can do for you; ask what you can do for your country.'
John F Kennedy

'Duty – Honour – Country. Those three hallowed words reverently dictate what you *ought* to be ...what you *can* be ... what you *will* be ... The unbelievers will say they are but words, but a slogan, but a flamboyant phrase.'
Douglas MacArthur

'I have a dream ...'
Martin Luther King

'The greatest leader of our time has been struck down by the foulest deed of our time. Today, John Fitzgerald Kennedy lives on in the immortal words and works he left behind. He lives on in the minds and memories of mankind. He lives on in the hearts of his countrymen.'

'No words are sad enough to express our sense of loss. No words are strong enough to express our determination to continue the forward thrust of America that he began.'
Lyndon B. Johnson

Words that motivate

Most people fall into three groups: visual, auditory or kinaesthetic (touch). They respond best to words that link into their personal channel of influence. This topic is covered in detail in books on NLP (Neuro Linguistic Programming), so I shall not attempt to do so here. However, here are a few examples of the words that work for each of the main groups.

Visual: Picture, bright, colour, look, black, vision, scene, vivid, visualise, imagine, see, perspective, clarify, insight, focus, shine.

Auditory: Loud, ring, clear, discuss, tell, quiet, say, hear, click, remark, rhythm, harmony, wavelength, dumb, call, tune.

Kinaesthetic: Soft, hard, rough, smooth, warmth, contact, rub, silky, sinuous, solid, scrape, firm, tangible, move.

These are the other categories and you can easily collect appropriate words and phrases for each:

Olfactory – influenced by the sense of smell: I smell a rat, this stinks of corruption, smelling of roses ...

Gustatory – influenced by the sense of taste: it leaves a bad taste in the mouth, bitter, sweet, sour, savour ...

Neutral – those who are guided by either reason or instinct: makes sense, gut feeling, can't argue, accept the case ...

◆ By using words from all groups, you include every member of the audience.
◆ You get yes responses by pressing the emotional buttons. You do that by using words that work.

Examples of evocative words:

(They won't all press your personal buttons)

engorge	enigmatic	dextrous	vanquish
irascible	vegetate	magnificent	crave
malleable	yearn	pulverise	cunning
gleaming	eloquent	plummet	shrewd
accentuate	impeccable	incessant	jocular
adamant	explosive	perceptive	muscular
sensual	steaming	bliss	gross

Add some of your own.

An exercise in imagination

Here's an exercise I came across some years ago.

> Read this little story aloud and then say what
> it means to you. Note that the story uses only
> seven different words. What's happening?
>
> 'Tramp, tramp. tramp, tramp, tramp.
> Rustle, rustle.
> Click. Aim.
> Fire!
> Thud.
> Silence.
> Tramp, tramp, tramp, tramp, tramp.'
>
> Try reading it out to a friends or colleagues
> and listen to what they tell you is happening.
> Is their interpretation the same as yours?
> Probably not.

What makes newspaper headlines work?

Let's consider a randomly chosen example. Here are a
couple of headlines that could have been written to signal
the return of Terry Venables to club football in England:

> Venables tipped to return to club football
>
> Venables is tempted to take the plunge at
> Riverside

The first states the facts. The second has several extra features. The word 'tempted' brings us closer to the decision-making process, and implies that the journalist has some inside knowledge of Terry's debate with himself. 'Take the plunge' is a popular phrase that also has emotional connections, implying an element of risk. Finally 'at Riverside' makes the story specific to one particular football club (Middlesbrough, whose ground is at Riverside). The first headline works well enough, but the second works far better because all those extra elements pack the second headline with more meaning as well as emotional appeal.

My love affair with words

Words have power. The right words can move grown men to tears and mobs to revolution. They can enthuse, inspire, and motivate your audience far more than facts alone – even if they happen to be German, whose preference for facts is legendary.

As a wordsmith I have an on-going love affair with words. It began at school. We had regular 'elocution' exams, for which we had to choose, memorise and deliver a poem or part of a play. At the age of 13 I chose Thomas Gray's 'Pindaric Ode' because of its powerful language, even though I did not fully understand all the words.

> 'Ruin seize thee, ruthless King !
> Confusion on thy banners wait !
> Tho' fann'd by Conquest's crimson wing
> They mock the air with idle state ...

—Such were the sounds that o'er the crested pride
Of the first Edward scatter'd wild dismay,
As down the steep of Snowdon's shaggy side
He wound with toilsome march his long array :—
Stout Glos'ter stood aghast in speechless trance ;
'To arms!' cried Mortimer, and couch'd his quivering
lance.'

There was more, much more, but I was intoxicated with
the images conjured up by those evocative, heroic words,
which I delivered at full volume and in a voice that
cracked at embarrassing moments. But I didn't care. I
had knights in armour to acclaim and Mortimer's
quivering lance to admire.

Shakespeare, the master of words that work

From there I graduated to Shakespeare, and in particular
to *Julius Caesar* which contains several memorable
speeches, including the most persuasive speech in
literature, in which Mark Antony turns a hostile crowd
into his instruments for revenge. He starts by asking for
a hearing, saying, 'Friends, Romans, countrymen, lend
me your ears' and leads them to pity him his grief over
the death of his friend, Caesar.

He appeals to their self-interest by revealing that Caesar
had included them in his will, and fans their emotions by
picking up Caesar's blood-stained robe and saying,

'If you have tears, prepare to shed them now.'
Finally, he is self-deprecating as he claims,

'I come not, friends, to steal away your hearts :
I am no orator, as Brutus is;
But, as you know me all, a plain blunt man
That loved my friend.'

The crowd rushes away to find Brutus and the rest, and
Mark Antony mutters,

'Now let it work. Mischief thou art afoot.
Take thou what course thou wilt.'

Mark Antony's sequence of persuasion

It took me quite a few years to realise the power in that
speech and in the structure of its persuasiveness.
Shakespeare lets Mark Antony:

◆ gain acceptance by denying that he is a threat of any
sort

◆ counter the argument by saying he doesn't disagree,
but providing evidence to the contrary

◆ win the sympathy vote by asking for their indulgence
as he pauses to cope with his personal grief

◆ appeal to the crowd's self interest by revealing Caesar's
will

◆ engage and expand their interest by appearing to
change his mind about the contents of the will

◆ inflame their emotions but take no credit for doing so

◆ downplay his own role as merely the messenger of the
truth

◆ get the action he wanted by finally revealing Caesar's
generosity, so that the crowd feel they have a personal
stake in seeking revenge.

Influences from schooldays

Sometimes we are influenced in ways we do not realise, by words we use and hear but whose power we do not recognise. My sister-in-law was praising me once for my helpfulness, and a portion of my old school song sprang to my mind:

> 'Here's a hand to a faltering brother,
> Here's a lift for the lame and the slow.
> And we'll stand, boys, like men for each other
> As onward through life we go.'

Those words seem to encapsulate all that I had been taught at school about helping others. To this day I get a lump in my throat when I sing that first line, and I applaud the genius of the Jesuit who wrote them so many years ago, when social values were so different.

Another set of words that gets me right here comes from Les Brown, the celebrated and immensely talented American motivational speaker. He tells the story of the man who first showed belief in him and who became his mentor, a teacher named Leroy Washington. I shall not tell the full story here, because I think you should hear Les Brown tell it in his own way. But the important part is where Mr Washington instructed the young Les Brown to write something on the blackboard, and Les demurred, saying, 'I can't do that, sir, I'm EMR (educable mentally retarded).'

Mr Washington rose and came out from behind his desk and told him, 'Don't ever let me hear you say that again. Someone else's opinion of you does not have to become your reality.'

I must have listened to the tape a hundred times, and I have even heard Les tell that story in person. Yet it never fails to tug at my heartstrings. The words themselves are simple ones, but the idea they contain is truly powerful. It's a message for self-reliance, a guideline for life.

Someone else's opinion of you does not have to become your reality.

It can pay to be brutally honest

Often the words that work best are those that convey an attitude that is refreshingly different. In the sixties, the London estate agent, Roy Brooks, made his name by filling his property ads with brutally honest descriptions. Not for him the mealy-mouthed phrases that required interpretation. Where others might have written 'a house of character' he would probably have said 'it needs a lot of hard work'. His ads openly stated that he thought some owners were asking too much for property that, in his opinion, had been largely ruined by their dogs. Yet he gained a cult following and sold houses almost as fast as he could get them on his books.

In similar vein, one man advertised his car for sale in these words: 'This car is a bitch. She smokes like a chimney and drinks like a fish.' He sold the car.

In Summary ...

◆ Use words that touch the heart.
◆ Remember the three gateways: Visual, Auditory, Kinaesthetic.
◆ Craft your sentences so that they have rhythm.
◆ Use such devices as contrasting pairs, groups of three and repetition.
◆ Use the words of everyday language, but include evocative ones.
◆ Use language that conveys your meaning most directly.

Never forget that your purpose is to create change, to stimulate, motivate and persuade.

Chapter 8

Opening: Objective and Hook

In this Chapter:

◆ **Should you open with a joke?**

◆ **Start with the end in view**

◆ **5 questions to sharpen your focus**

◆ **The vital hook**

◆ **Examples of attention getters.**

Many a book on public speaking recommends starting with a joke. To me, that advice comes from the days when travelling salesmen wore bow ties and told jokes for a living. Bad jokes.

In fact, it reminds me of the old joke (which I'm sure you've heard a hundred times before) of the (American) bigwig who went abroad and addressed an audience who could not speak a word of English. He opened with a joke that took about 40 seconds to tell. The interpreter then spoke for about five seconds, and the audience all hooted with laughter. The bigwig was amazed and asked the interpreter what he'd said. The interpreter replied, 'I said, foreign bigshot told funny story. Everybody laugh.'

I first read that story in *Reader's Digest* a number of years ago. I read it again mid-2000, when it was sent in by a reader and published as one of their 'Laughter' stories. I'm amazed the *Reader's Digest* filter failed to recognise and exclude it. Or perhaps the magazine's editors put it in themselves, pretending that it came from a reader. Either way, *I* remembered it, and that affected my regard for the magazine.

How is that relevant to your own public utterances? Its relevance is to warn you of the dangers of following the old advice about opening with a joke. The dangers are these:

◆ the joke may not be new to the listener
◆ you may not be a practised joke teller
◆ if the joke falls flat, it may affect your standing with your listener
◆ if the joke is irrelevant to your subject, it may simply irritate.

Let me stress that this is not to say that you should never open with a joke. Sometimes an apt joke would be an ideal way to start, all the more so if you can adapt it to suit the occasion and perhaps relate it to someone who is present.

> On one occasion, when I arrived as the principal speaker at an anniversary dinner of a well-known organisation, I mentioned to the Chairman that it was my birthday. He told me that they held the annual dinner in the same week of every year, and that one of their members, called Nick, usually claimed it was in honour of his birthday, which fell at about the

same date as mine. It was a natural
opportunity to hijack Nick's joke, and when I
rose to speak I duly thanked the members for
coming to celebrate my birthday, and even for
paying to be there. I then added, 'Eat your
heart out, Nick!' and everyone roared with
laughter because they recognised the 'in-joke'.

Your starting point

Before you utter a single word, and even before you plan
what you are going to say, you need to be clear about
your objective. What do you want to achieve?

◆ Start with the end in mind.
◆ What outcome do you want?
◆ If you are making a presentation, remember that your
  purpose should be to bring about change – in the
  thinking, attitude or behaviour of your listeners.
◆ If you are addressing a single person, you should
  similarly want to bring about some change in the
  situation.
  – It could be to make the other person better disposed
  towards you.
  – It may be to improve his/her knowledge or skills.
  – It could be to get approval for a contract, or for you
  to marry his son or daughter.

Whatever the purpose, you need to clarify your own
thinking about your objective, by asking and answering
some basic questions.

I once took over a sales force that was (supposed to be) selling advertising on a national newspaper. I put it like that because all they were doing was imposing their (often indifferent) personalities on their prospects. They had no idea why they were calling, or what their purpose should have been. The sales management strategy I adopted was to make the salesmen aware of their objective, and that in turn made them more interesting to their prospects.

I told them never to go into a meeting with any client or prospect without having the answers to five questions on the tips of their tongues. If they did not have the answers ready, they were not to go in. 'If necessary,' I said, 'walk around the block and find the answers. Then, and only then, are you entitled to go in.'

What were the questions? Here they are:

1. Why am I here?
2. Why should he or she see me?
3. What can I offer that he or she can't get from someone else?
4. What do I want at the end of this meeting?
5. What's the least I'll settle for?

Let's consider the relevance and importance of each question.

1. Why am I here?
Seems obvious, doesn't it? Well, how would *you* answer it? Suppose you were waiting in reception, and your

managing director walked in, quite by chance, and asked you that question. There are glib answers, fumbling ones, and there is the right one. Does your answer reflect your own importance in the exchange? Does it place the right value on your expertise and time? Think about it.

The answer to this question establishes what *you* bring to the party.

2. Why should he see me?

Let me re-phrase that: Why should he feel that he must see me? If it is out of politeness, or because you are imposing on an existing relationship, the ice is very thin and you are certain to fall in. Think of it like this: suppose you have made an appointment and you are waiting in reception. Your prospect appears, clutching his diary and full of apologies. 'Terribly sorry,' he says, 'I'm double-booked. My fault entirely. Could we re-schedule?'

'Of course,' you reply, 'no trouble at all.' And you reach for you own diary. Then he says, 'Just remind me ... what are we going to be talking about?'

If you do not have a compelling reply on the tip of your tongue, he's more than likely to say, 'Tell you what, why don't you call me in a month or so and we'll fix something.' Guess what that means. It means, 'So long, farewell, goodbye ... for ever!' You've blown it!

The answer to this question will determine if you are entitled to a hearing, whether it's as a salesman or as a presenter. It's the answer to the WIIFM question: What's In It For Me? It presents the main benefit. In the elevator speech, it's the solution you provide to the problem that you first articulate, and which gets the other person nodding in agreement.

3. What can I offer that he can't get from someone else?

This is, of course, about your USP – your Unique Selling Proposition.

A client of mine devised a clever way of integrating data collected from a diversity of sources, and making a simple summary available as needed. However, in their marketing they did not make anything of that integration process. When I pointed out that they were overlooking their own USP, they seemed surprised. They said that the technology was available for anyone in their field to do what they did, so it was not strictly unique. By adopting that attitude they were denying themselves a strong marketing advantage.

A USP does not have to be absolutely unique. It can be the one thing that makes you or your proposition stand apart from others in your field.

4. What do I want at the end of this meeting?

The first time I faced a salesman with this question, he gave me a glib answer. He said, 'An order, of course.' So I asked him where his order book was. He said he didn't usually carry one because he accepted verbal orders which his customers could confirm with one of their own orders.

Would *you* do business like that? It's all right to make the occasional exception, but just consider how many hostages to fortune that salesman was offering. Verbal orders are:

(a) easy to forget
(b) easy to get wrong
(c) easy to cancel
(d) often incomplete
(e) impossible to challenge when things go wrong.

Relying on customers or clients to confirm the order in writing imposes a responsibility and an administrative task on them that they may resent. In this salesman's line of work, it would have been perfectly normal to produce an order book, complete the agreed details, then ask for a signature. By including the order at the end of the formal presentation, the salesman had a focus, and clearly signalled to the client that he was there to do business, not merely to conduct a conversation.

When you make a presentation, formal or otherwise, your purpose is to take people from where they are to where you want them to be. This requires persuasion, and you need something to indicate that your persuasion has achieved your objective.

5. What's the least I'll settle for?
If you have an objective, you will want to achieve it. Of course, it is always possible that sometimes you will not manage to persuade others to your point of view. That can result in a feeling of rejection, and rejection hurts.

Plan a fall-back option. If you cannot achieve your main objective, is there some lesser objective that will keep the door open for another time ... and allow you to keep your tail up as well? It could be another appointment, a referral to some other person who might be more interested in your proposition or even a clear statement of the reason for not accepting your proposition. This last is a valuable way to get back and try again.

With one sales force that I managed, at the end of each sales call, if a sale had not been made, the salesman had to write down the *one* objection he had not been able to answer. They laughed behind my back when I explained the acronym on their report sheets: MONATT. It stood for Main Objection Not Answered This Time. They laughed at first. But they soon realised that by asking for the right feedback at the end of each unsuccessful call, they had a reason to go back again when they had found a way of overcoming that objection.

What was the result of adopting this approach to selling advertising? We **tripled** revenue in just ten months.

Let me now turn to the hook

The hook is the attention-grabber that you use at the start. In my 30-second story I used the image of the attractive blonde in a red dress as my hook. In press ads and newspaper stories the headline is the hook. It stops you by saying, 'Look at this! It's for you!'

The hook is a vital ingredient in any persuasive communication. It should therefore offer a benefit for listening, a benefit that is specific to the person or people you are addressing.

> When I prepared to address the inaugural meeting of the Professional Speakers Association of Europe, I asked myself what would interest a room full of professional speakers and wannabe speakers. I asked myself what drives someone to become a professional speaker. Two things: ego and money. Since most of them were already attending to the first, I decided to focus on the second.
>
> I held up a long piece of paper on which I printed a very large sum of money: $38,000,000,000. On the reverse I had printed £24,000,000,000. I said,
>
> 'This year, Americans will pay 38 billion dollars to hear someone speak. I'll translate that into English: they will pay 24 billion pounds to hear someone speak. That's two billion pounds every month, 500 million pounds every week of the year. To hear someone speak.'

Every person in the room was silently saying, 'I want some of that!' I had their complete attention.

How do you decide on your own hook? Ask yourself these questions:

◆ What's the main benefit of what you are going to say?
◆ What's the most unusual aspect of your subject?
◆ What makes your topic 'different'?
◆ What's most amusing about it?
◆ What's in it for them?
◆ What's a 'hot button' for this audience?

See if you can answer each question in a single sentence that's no longer than this one. Then phrase it like a headline. In my example above, my hook sentence was:

'This year, Americans will pay 38 billion dollars to hear someone speak.'

Follow the example of newspapers (usually tabloids are best for this). See how direct their headlines are ... and how they pack in information wrapped up in emotive terms. Here are a few examples:

Race to be first to reach stricken yacht

Marathon summit in chaos

How will digital shape advertising on the airwaves?

Property family to face a backlash over buyback plan

Free offer to schools puts BBC in bad books

Press advertisements are also good sources of headlines, like these:

> Introducing the latest breakthrough in mortgage reduction: your current account.

> Retired homeowner? Read about an extra income for life from your home.

> Cash if you die, cash if you don't.

> New exclusive mortgage opportunity for Company Directors and Self Employed.

> Will you realise the benefits of AA membership ... by accident?

And here's one from a classified ad selling a house:

> Two loos, no trek

Each headline has its own cleverness. All are succinct, clear and well-directed. They signal their subject matter to the relevant section of the passing parade of readers. Some are intriguing, others pose a rhetorical question that may find an echo in the minds of some readers. Some are plain, others use puns or other linguistic tricks to catch the eye and encourage repetition.

Ask yourself what you find appealing about the ones you like, and apply similar reasoning to creating your own hook.

In summary ...

◆ Don't try to be a comedian. Unless you are one.

◆ Be clear about the outcome you want to achieve.

◆ Use the 5 questions to quiz yourself about your purpose.

◆ Make your hook startling, amazing or unexpected, but keep it relevant.

◆ Headlines in tabloids and press ads are useful examples of attention getters.

Chapter 9

Structure

In this Chapter:

- **how structure helps you make your point**
- **simple structures for every occasion**
- **PREP**
- **past/present/future**
- **problem/cause/solution**
- **tell x 3**
- **how to be ready to 'say a few words'.**

Suppose you were at an event such as a celebratory dinner or a retirement party for a colleague, and without warning the chairman or host turned to you and said, 'Come on, say a few words.' How would you feel? Most people would freeze, dry up or ramble on, knowing that they were not giving the best account of themselves. Has it ever happened to you? Have you ever dried on your feet?

It can happen to anyone. I was in a speech contest once, and up against four others, including the reigning champion, whom I shall call James. I spoke before him and delivered a speech full of passion and conviction on an issue of current importance in Britain. During my speech, James decided to change his prepared speech, possibly to match my performance. A little while later, it was his turn.

He started well, with an apple as his hook. He set the scene, bit into the apple and made some point about it ... then faltered and stopped. Reaching ˏ his pocket, he pulled out the scrap of paper on which he had scribbled some words during my speech, but he couldn't make sense of them up there on the platform, under the spotlight, in the heat of the competition. He spoke another few words, completely lost his drift, and stopped again. He apologised and sat down. He had dried in mid-competition.

Why people dry up

What is it that causes people to dry up when the spotlight is on them? Is it because they have nothing to say? Oddly enough, the opposite is true. It's because they don't know how to choose from the many things they might want to say.

I believe that James ground to a halt in the competition because the last-minute thoughts he added to his prepared speech shifted the focus away from his original intention. He didn't have time to integrate them into the flow of argument he had originally planned, and he ended up trying to remember specific words rather than the point he wanted to make.

What would have helped? In a word, **structure**.

Structure tells you what to say first, what to lead up to, and what to say next. Structure lets you buy time on your feet because you don't have to worry about the relevance of what you are saying. Just follow the prescribed sequence and you will stay on track. The simple structures I am going to take you through now will help you deal with impromptu speaking and with question and answer sessions, and also help you develop an argument within a prepared speech or presentation. They can even be used as the overall structure of a 40-minute keynote address or presentation.

PREP

Suppose you are asked to 'say a few words' or express your opinion during a group discussion, and without any warning. Here's one way to acquit yourself with distinction. Use the universal structure PREP.

Here's how it works:

Position: This is what I think.
Reason: Here's why I think that.
Example: Here's how it works in practice.
Position: That's why I think what I think.

Let's apply that to a real-life question. Let's say you were asked to 'tell us what you think about commuting to work by train'. This could be your answer:

Position: I think commuting by train has become an ordeal that imposes an unacceptably high level of stress on those who have to travel that way every day. And I believe that it must be remedied without delay.

Reason: I say that because there is severe overcrowding, resulting in passengers having to stand throughout the journey, often packed like sardines, breathing foul air. The service is no longer reliable, with trains that are often late and even subject to cancellation at a moment's notice.

Example: Let me illustrate that with two examples, one from each end of the scale. On the one hand you have fairly junior office workers whose advancement within the firm might be hindered if they are often late into work. On the other hand you might have someone on her way to a meeting with a prospective new client who can only manage a breakfast meeting. Her train is cancelled and she arrives half an hour late. The meeting is aborted and she loses the business.

Position: Those are fairly typical situations in which commuters find themselves, and I think it is unacceptable on social and on commercial grounds. That's why I say that it must be remedied without delay.

PREP is appropriate whenever you are asked to state your opinion or position, or when you have strong feelings on the subject. 'This is what I think ... here's why ... here's an example ... that's why I think it.'

A variation is when you want to make a proposal, and the P then stands for Proposition rather than Position.

Like this:

Proposition: This what I'd like you to do.

Reason: Here's why.

Example: Here's how it would work for you.

Proposition: That's why I want you to do it.

When would it be right to use this structure? Well, think of a board meeting when the chair suddenly turn to you and asks, 'What do you think we should do?' Or when you want to persuade someone to take on some task or responsibility. You might say:

I really think you should be in charge of the next Annual Conference.
I say that because you have the energy, the persuasiveness, and the organisational skills.
For example, I was very impressed with the way you organised that meeting for those visiting Americans at short notice.
That's why I believe you are the right person to run the Annual Conference.

Note how the structure actually helps you to be brief, because you do not have to ramble while you search for something meaningful to say. The structure tells you what to say, and when. Moving on, let's consider some other simple structures to get you out of trouble or off to a flying start.

Past, present, future

The simplest structure, and the one with the widest application, is 'past, present, future'. Here's how it works:

'This is how things used to be ... this is how they are at present ... here's what might happen in the future.'

Of course, you might choose a more elaborate form of words, such as:

'Let's first consider the historical perspective ... now let's consider where we have got to ... now let's consider the options available to us.'

The past: It's easy because you can look back as far or as recently as you choose. Perhaps you were there at the time of the events you are describing and can add your personal perceptions. It is, however, important to draw lessons from the past that you are describing, and show how the events of the past have led to the current situation.

The present: Talking about the present day is easy because you are here, you can see what's happening and you know what you think about either the inadequacies or the advantages of the current situation. While you are talking about the present, you will usually find that it helps you to decide what to say about the future.

The future: As you look ahead and consider the options available to you, your speculation is as valid as the next person's. If you link it to what you have already said about the past and the present, it will hang together well and provide a logical sequence of events, justifying your point of view about the future.

EXAMPLE: Talk about London Transport, using past, present, future.

In the distant past, Londoners travelled on foot, on horseback or in horse-drawn carriages. The average speed of travel by horse-power was a sedate 10mph. Then things got better with the introduction of the motor car, bicycles and, later, trams, buses and tube trains. During the 50s and 60s, public transport in London was convenient, reliable and cheap.

Today, things are very different. The streets are clogged with too many cars, and public transport is overcrowded, unreliable and expensive. It is not a viable alternative to the private car, and the average speed of road journeys through central London has dropped to a mere 8mph – slower than in the 19th century. And recently, the *Evening Standard* revealed that, through sheer mismanagement, London Transport dissipated £10 billion that should have been spent on improving the service.

The question is, what will happen in the future? What is likely to happen to London Transport in the years ahead?

In my opinion, the entire management structure of London Transport's several wings should be fired, and a new team put in place, to run the system like a proper business. The first priority must be to offer a viable alternative to the private car. The way forward might be to integrate all transport systems across the capital, with a lower fare structure to tempt Londoners back.

More tube trains, more frequent overland trains, shorter bus routes, with improved cleanliness and comfort – those are essential requirements. In short, facilities must improve, with a more reliable service and greater safety for passengers. Only then will there be an incentive to leave the car at home.

That's about two minutes' worth, and it closely follows the prescribed sequence of past, present, future. The bold sentences signal each section, to keep the listeners on track and let them know what's coming next.

Problem, cause, solution

The structure that best suits business situations is 'problem, cause, solution':

> This is what's wrong.
> Here's how it came about.
> This is what we can do about it.

You have probably spotted that it is past, present, future in a different order. The problem is the present, the cause is the past, and the solution is the future. However, it is not just a different sequence – the emphasis is not the same. Here the focus is on a specific difficulty rather than a strategy based on a chronological sequence.

This is an ideal structure for Q & A sessions, or for politicians being interviewed on television. It provides the opportunity to think about the right answer to give while re-stating the problem. Or, by redefining the problem it ensures that your answer can be on your own terms.

Here's an example of how you might use this structure:

1. **Problem:** Let's be clear about the problem. Bookings for our seminars are falling off and we are wringing our hands about the effectiveness of our marketing programme. However, I believe that the real problem lies in the way we are handling the enquiries we are getting. Let us put on one side, for the moment, the question of our marketing, and recognise that we are losing too many of those who respond to our advertising, just by the way we handle their enquiries.

2. **Cause:** The reason why we lose so many people after their first contact is that incoming calls have always been handled by anyone in the office. If the phone rings, the nearest person answers it. If it is someone calling in response to an ad, and a non-salesperson answers, he or she might simply say, 'Give me your name and address and I'll get someone to send you details of our next seminar.'

3. **Solution:** The solution lies in training. Ideally, our telesales staff should handle all enquiries, and they must be trained to treat every call as a conversion oppportunity. However, I believe that every member of staff should also be trained, so that they can all act as ambassadors for the company, and keep every enquiry alive until a salesperson is available to conduct the scripted telephone interview.

4. **Action:** We should therefore ask PKP Communicators to propose a suitable programme of training for both sales and non-sales staff.

Clearly, points 1 to 3 follow the structure, but I have added the all-important fourth point: Action. When you've defined the problem, identified the cause and suggested the solution, should you just leave the matter hanging in the air, expecting some change to take place by itself? Or should you propose a specific course of action to implement the solution that you have just proposed.

Remember, the purpose in making a presentation, however brief, is to bring about change, and that requires action. Never rely on your listeners to make the connection between agreeing with you and taking the next step. Tell them what to do.

Tell x 3

This structure is extremely well-known, but it needs to be included because it works so well and helps the communication process more than most. Tell x 3 simply stands for:

1. Tell 'em what you're going to tell 'em.
2. Tell 'em.
3. Tell 'em what you've told 'em.

This structure can stand alone or it can be combined with any of the others. When used on its own, here's how it can work:

Tell 1: When we come to talk about the influence of television on our children, I think we should look at their viewing habits, at whether television gets in the way of more useful things, whether television distorts the values of our children, and finallly what we can do to stop the rising tide.

Tell 2: Let's start by considering viewing habits of the younger generation. They switch on the box when they enter a room and switch it off when they leave. It's a constant accompaniment to whatever else they are doing.

Does it get in the way of better things? Clearly it does. The time spent watching television is time taken from other things. It is also many times greater than the time spent by previous generations at the cinema.

Children see events and relationships that distort the values they may have been taught at home or at school, and they are often presented with powerful role models whose inappropriate attitudes and behaviour they copy.

In addition, the mere fact of having the TV on all the time must interfere with their capacity to think creatively or to commune with themselves.

The only way to counter this trend is for parents to limit TV watching to specific programmes and to determine a maximum number of hours per day or week. Because such a course of action will be difficult, it should be backed by a government-sponsored publicity campaign, such as the ones for Aids awareness and against smoking and drug-taking.

Tell 3: In conclusion, let me repeat that this is a difficult problem arising out of the unrestrained viewing habits of the younger generation. As I said, I believe there are strong and undesirable behaviour models in TV programmes, and I believe that the government should encourage parents to limit and control the viewing habits of their children.

Tell x 3 can also be used together with one of the other structures. For example, you might say:

'I propose to tackle this by first considering the
    background (past),
then looking at where we are and what's wrong with the
    current situation (present),
before making my proposals for change (future).'

That's tell 1.

In tell 2 you cover the subject as indicated, i.e. past, present, future.

In tell 3 you summarise by saying something like:

'So, it's plain that the poor practices of the past have led to the current weaknesses in the system. Going forward, we have two options available to us, and I favour the second.'

In summary ...

♦ **People 'dry' in mid speech if they lose track of what they are trying to say.**

♦ **Simple structures keep you on track.**

♦ **Structures make you think and guide your choice of what to say.**

♦ **The simple structures shown here can be used in isolation or in combination.**

♦ **When you have to speak impromptu, or when handling a Q & A session, these structures will help you to cope impressively.**

Eight Things to Do

In this Chapter:

◆ **Focus on the right objective.**

◆ **Start with a powerful hook.**

◆ **Remember who your audience is.**

◆ **Be clear about your core message.**

◆ **Build up their interest.**

◆ **Follow a structure.**

◆ **Don't forget a call to action.**

◆ **Stand and deliver like a true professional.**

Let me offer you eight things to do, if you want to communicate effectively. We have already considered some of the basic principles of persuasive communication, and identified some of the obstacles to effective communication. Let us now think about the positive things to do if you want to put your point across clearly and succinctly.

The eight that I shall focus on are contained in the acronym:

OH AM I SAD

... because you *will* be sad if you ignore them. Because then you are unlikely to achieve your purpose.

O is for Outcome or Objective

When you are preparing a presentation or even a statement, always start with the end in mind. What do you want to achieve? What change do you want to bring about?

How do you identify your objective? Start by asking yourself some questions:

◆ Why am I making this speech/presentation?
◆ What change do I want to make in their thinking or behaviour as a result?
◆ What action do I want them to take?
◆ Why should they listen to me?
◆ How will they benefit?

Imagine you were talking to a child. You know you cannot make a speech to a child because children have a low attention span, especially when grown-ups are telling them 'something serious'. Their eyes wander, they shuffle their feet, they soon say, 'Can I go now, please?' So you have to get to the point and tell them in a sentence or two what you want them to know or do.

Use the same approach in defining your objective.

The objective, by definition, is what you are aiming at. It's what you want to achieve. So you need to be specific about what it is and by what means or by which route you intend to get there. That means you must think through both steps:

- what you want to achieve
- how you want to get there.

Bad objectives:

- Passive: to communicate information.
- Unspecific: to improve performance.
- Too many: to strengthen the client relationship, to tell them who we are and what we do, and to encourage them to give us more work.
- Self-centred: to impress.
- Vague: to network.
- Unfocused: to present our credentials.

Good objectives:

- To propose how we would solve their problem.
- To present an Action Plan that will increase productivity by at least 10 per cent a year.
- To demonstrate how we would improve response to their advertising.
- To persuade them to adopt and implement our programme.

H is for Hook

The hook is the thing that grabs attention, like the headline in an advertisement. It's a vital – and even essential – ingredient.

The hook says, 'Stop! This is for YOU!'

Think of the trailers for news programmes on television or radio, or 'cliffhangers' just before commercial breaks. They tell you what's coming next, briefly outlining the main attraction so that you are hooked and stay tuned. Examples:

> 'Coming up in the six o'clock news ... even more shocking news of the mounting total of killings by Britain's worst ever serial killer. And why motorists are switching to smaller cars. Also, what Madonna said to the Spice Girls at her wedding. All that in the news at six o'clock, but first ...'

> 'With the score standing level at 15 all, it's been a cracking semi-final first half and it promises to be an even more spectacular second half. Just before they resume, we'll be getting a view on what the coaches might have said in the two dressing rooms during half time to get their players to raise their game even higher. That's in a couple of minutes, right after the break. Stay tuned.'

The hook can take many forms. Some people believe in opening with a joke. That's fine if it works, and humour is a good hook.

A quotation is a powerful hook, and so is some example from your personal experience. Another good hook is a relevant reference to someone important in your audience, perhaps in a friendly, mocking way. Whatever your choice, use it to capture the attention of your listeners and provide the springboard for your message.

A is for Audience

Who is listening? Make your pitch relevant and appropriate.

The hook you select should be specific to the audience you will be addressing, and take account of their needs and interests. If there are women present, it would be sensible to avoid saying 'he' and 'him' in all your examples, and avoid making jokes that might give offence. If there are people from other countries, do take account of the cultural and linguistic differences. For those whose first language is not the same as yours, you do need to speak more slowly, and to pause often, to enable them to take in what you are saying.

> One occasion when I got it badly wrong was in the Anglo-Irish final of the International Speech Contest in 1994. Although it was held in England on that occasion, there were more Irish contestants than English, and therefore more Irish judges as well.
>
> I made a patriotic speech called 'Who are the Winners?' in which I spoke about putting the 'Great' back into Britain by restoring the traditional values that had helped Britain to win the Second World War.

Although many members of the audience thought I had made the best speech, I did not even place in the first three, because the Irish judges had felt offended and decided that I had not taken account of the Irish presence in the hall. One of the Irish judges (whom I had previously counted as a friend) even told me later that she had been 'very angry' at the content of my speech. A rather strong reaction, I thought, but a reminder of the importance of considering who will be listening, and what their stance might be.

M is for Message

Your core message – it's what you want people to remember after you have gone.

When you start your preparations, the very first thing to write down is your core message. It is also the last thing to write when you have completed your preparations. Write it first as a statement of what you intend to put across. Write it again at the end because as you develop your case the emphasis might shift, or you may even realise that your actual message is different from the one you first thought of.

The way to focus on your core message is to think about people going away after hearing you speak. Someone arrives late and asks, 'What was that about?' What would you like the answer to be? What would you like people to carry away and remember about what you said?

That's your core message. You should be able to state it in a sentence or two.

The core message could be expresssed as your hook. It will certainly influence the thrust of your argument. And, when you are putting your point across in just a minute or less, it could be your entire message.

I is for Interest

It's your build up, the process by which you take your listeners to the point of desire, when they say 'I want that.'

Your hook has grabbed the attention of your audience. If it was a good hook, it sharply raised their interest, but not enough to reach the level of acceptance, so you must continue to build their interest by piling on benefits. Remember, you have to overcome their existing way of thinking in an attractive, persuasive way. Show the benefits of thinking *your* way. Only when those benefits far outweigh the comfort of their current thinking will they be prepared to make the change you want to bring about.

I said 'far outweigh' because there is always a price to pay when people make a change. Your way has to offer a much better deal, and it must appeal to their self-interest.

S is for Structure

Structure is what keeps you on track and lets your listeners follow you more easily.

Chapter 10 takes you through several simple structures that can be used in short statements even complete keynote speeches or presentations.

A is for Action

If you want to bring about change, what do your listeners have to do to get what you are proposing? Don't leave them guessing.

Most often, the call to action comes at or very near the end, but it can sometimes be stated early on, when the whole of the speech or presentation will be a justification of that call. You might say:

'I want you to take positive action in your town, in your community, in your street, to eradicate this menace. There are things that every one of you can do, and should do. I'll tell you what those things are and what you need to do first to make sure they work for you. But first, let me explain why we must all take action ...'

If your call to action comes at the end, make sure the action you propose is easy to understand and to implement. **Make the initial commitment a small and simple one.** Then it can lead to something bigger. If the commitment is too big, or one that requires thought, your chances of success are slim.

Be specific. Don't ask people to 'try harder' or 'pull together for a better society' and 'all do our bit for the planet'. Tell them to:

'Buy this book and focus on Chapter 10, which is about Managing Change in Business. Do the things it recommends. You can start tomorrow. You can make changes that will create a happier and healthier working environment. Your staff will enjoy coming to work more than ever before. They will become more productive. Your business will prosper. And you will set an example for other businesses to follow. The nation will benefit, and so, eventually, will the planet.'

That kind of approach is specific in its recommendations, specific in the local benefits that will result, and specific in the wider levels of knock-on benefits.

D is for Delivery

Your message may be terrific, and you may be full of conviction. You may have put together a powerful argument, full of great facts and ideas, but the success of your speech or presentation will largely depend on the way you put it across.

Conviction is a key element. It is hard to resist a person who speaks with passion and from the heart. If you believe in what you are saying and proposing, let that belief show.

You also need to develop a number of techniques to lift your performance above the ordinary. These are:

1. voice
2. pitch, pace and pauses
3. platform presence.

1. Voice:

A speaker with an attractive voice has a much greater chance of getting his or her ideas accepted. A good speaking voice should be easy on the ear, clear and loud enough to be heard without strain, expressive and able to touch the emotions of the listener.

The essentials of a good speaking voice are indicated by the word ADVANCE. As sentries used to say: advance and be recognised !

Audible: loud enough to be heard without effort and well-projected.

Distinct: clear, with end-consonants sounded, and space between words.

Varied: expressive, conveying shades of meaning and changes of pace.

Agreeable: friendly and approachable, not tight or tense.

Natural: sincere, not self-conscious, as though you are talking to friends.

Concordant: the opposite of discordant, i.e. pleasant or musical on the ear.

Energetic: carrying vitality, conviction and enthusiasm.

2. Pitch, pace and pauses

These are the variables that add variety and interest to a speech or presentation.

Pitch: the key in which you speak, or the main note that is heard. Find the right starting note, so that you sound authoritative and natural, and feel comfortable. Beware the tendency to go too high. The larger the audience, the greater the temptation to strain and raise the pitch.

Practise speaking into a tape recorder, playing back with the volume turned down, to decide if it sounds attractive. Try recording the same passage at several different pitches.

Try switching to a different pitch (usually lower) in mid speech, for dramatic effect.

Pace: the speed at which you speak should also be varied. The ideal range is between 120 and 160 words per minute. The more energy you put into your speaking the slower you will be, even if it doesn't feel that way.

Speaking too slowly and deliberately sounds pompous. Speaking too quickly can cause words to be swallowed, and for them to run into each other. It can give the impression that you are speaking for your own benefit rather than for the benefit of your listeners.

To give the impression of high pace, without losing clarity, hit the end consonants of your words.

Pauses: Take your time and do not gabble.

Use the pause for dramatic effect, and to allow your point to sink in.

You should pause:

◆ at the start, to get attention
◆ between main points, as punctuation, and to let your listeners know that you have completed the previous point
◆ before a significant piece of information
◆ before the punch line of a joke.

Vary the pattern of the whole speech. Vary the pattern of each section. Vary the pattern of separate paragraphs.

Variety keeps your listeners interested, and signals your willingness to communicate.

3. Platform presence

1. Speak with conviction and energy
- Don't hold back. You have only *this* opportunity to persuade. How would you speak if you were in desperate trouble and you were addressing the one person who could do you the favour that would get you out of trouble?

2. Be focused
- Facts tell, feelings sell! Remember that your objective is to persuade others to your point of view.

They must *want* to make the change, and that derives from emotion rather than reason. The latter only justifies the emotional decision.

3. Make it a performance
- Use drama, images, visual aids. Every speech or presentation should be delivered as a performance, enhanced by such visual aids as are necessary to enliven the message and enthuse the audience.

4. Be distinctive
- Make it memorable. Put your personal mark on it. Develop a personal style and a 'signature story' that people associate with you, and which they will come to expect whenever you present.

5. Use vocal variety
- Entertain and surprise them. Keep them interested. No-one has the right to be boring! See the section earlier in this chapter for detailed recommendations on vocal variety.

6. Have empathy
- Talk *to* them, not *at* them. Don't fear personal contact. Look people in the eye, feel their response, stay with them a little longer when you see them agreeing with you or identifying with your message. Smile and give them a reason to like you.

7. Maintain good eye contact
- Look at one friendly face at a time. As your eye sweeps over your audience, try to hold each person's

gaze for three seconds at some point. Start with a friendly face, and smile. That friendly face will smile back and that will lift your spirits and make you look even more friendly to the rest of the audience.

8. Show what you mean

- Use gestures and positive body language. *You* are the presentation and its main illustration. Your gestures should be smooth and relevant. Use your hands and arms to add meaning to what you are saying, not simply to beat time.

9. Stand tall and balanced

- Stay centred, walk with a purpose. How you stand and move will tell the audience how secure and authoritative you are. Authority adds stature. Remember how much bigger your school teachers looked when you were young, and how much smaller they seem now?

10. Serve the audience's needs

- Offer information, entertainment and involvement. Never forget that everyone is tuned into the same favourite radio station: WII FM – What's In It For Me? If they had a choice, they chose to come and listen to you because they had expectations. Think about those expectations and how you can meet them.

Finally, PRACTISE,
      PRACTISE,
            PRACTISE!

In summary ...

- ◆ **Know why you are speaking.**
- ◆ **Grab their attention with a hook.**
- ◆ **Make it relevant, benefit-laden and easy to follow.**
- ◆ **Give them a take-away message.**
- ◆ **Tell them how to get it.**
- ◆ **Develop professional speaking techniques.**

Chapter 11

Seven More Ideas for Great Speeches

In this Chapter:

♦ **three Ms: Message / Messenger / Method**
♦ **four Ks: Katch 'em / Keep 'em / Konvince 'em / Kore Message**
♦ **putting your point across in just a minute.**

To be a good communicator you must have a sense of mission. And mission consists of the three Ms:
♦ Message
♦ Messenger
♦ Method.

The three Ms concern you. The four Ks, which follow, concern your audience. All seven are prompts, to guide your thinking when you start to prepare a speech.

Mission

What do I mean by 'Mission'?

I mean what I wrote in Chapter 3 – you must want to bring about some change, otherwise why make the speech or presentation? That change could be something radical or it could be simply to make people aware of the significance of something they already know, so that they will take action.

Whether you are making a single speech for one particular occasion, or making speeches as a professional, you need a sense of purpose, or your speech will be not much more than an interlude. Making a speech need not be very difficult, but making a great speech requires rather more thought and preparation.

Because of my connection with the Professional Speakers Association, I am sometimes asked by wannabe speakers, 'What does it take to be a professional speaker?' My answer is always the same: 'It takes just three things. You must have something to say. You must really want to say it. Then you must develop the right techniques for putting it across.'

That's Message, Messenger, Method.

1. Message

The first requirement of any speaker is this: have something to say.

That's not as obvious as you might suppose. Think of the number of times you have listened to someone speak from a public platform and wondered, 'What's the point you are making?' or 'Could you get to the point?' That happens when the speaker does not have a clear idea of what he or she wants to say.

There are five ways to identify your message:

1. What's your speech title? Does it carry a sexy attraction that would persuade people to pay to hear you speak, and is that what you really want people to hear and to know?

2. Would you pay to hear you speak on that topic?

3. What's the sub-title of your speech? Does it describe the essential ingredient of your topic?

4. What do you want people to carry away in their minds and in their hearts long after you have finished speaking?

5. If someone approaches a member of your audience after you have finished, and asks what your speech had been about, what would you like the answer to be?

Ideally, all five tests should come up with the same answer.

Successful professional speakers concentrate on a very small number of topics, maybe as few as two or three. They make themselves expert on those topics, creating a niche for themselves, so that when you think of those topics you think of them, and when you think of them you think of those topics. They achieve that by concentrating on what they want to say about that topic, not on delivering a dissertation on the topic itself.

2. Messenger

Don't try to deliver the encyclopaedia. Focus on what *you* contribute to the topic, on what *you* know and believe about it, and on what belongs to *you*.

Question 2 above applies not only to the message but also to the messenger.

It's not about how clever your text is, nor about the relevance of the subject matter. It's about why it should be *you* speaking about it from this platform. What is it that you bring to the party? What can you tell the audience that they can't get (better) from some other speaker ... or from a book or article in a newspaper or magazine?

The message and the messenger are inextricably linked, because the 'something to say' must belong to you. It must come from the heart – *your* heart. And it must be the kind of message that is burning you up inside, keeping you awake at night, driving you to stand up and tell people about it. That's when your speech will be compelling and you will be irresistible!

Is it necessary to have such a powerful motivating force before you make a speech? Only if you want to make a difference when you speak. (Those who don't care if they make a difference can only be indifferent.)

Your role as messenger isn't just to deliver information. It is to touch the hearts of your hearers and change their lives.

3. Method

The third ingredient is method – the right techniques for doing justice to your message and putting it across in a way that takes your listeners from where they are to where you want them to be.

You need focus, you need structure, you need to follow the process of persuasion. Think about the 30-second example in Chapter 1 and practise the techniques for putting your point across in just a minute. I'll summarise them for you at the end of this chapter.

First, let me offer you the four Ks. They concern your relationship with the audience.

The four Ks

Katch 'em

This is a variation on the 'hook' theme. Before you can communicate, you must first grab the attention of the other person(s).

When making a prepared speech, you need to build in a hook, as detailed in Chapter 8.

When making an impromptu speech it's a little harder, but the idea is the same: say something unexpected but relevant to the topic. Think of it as the headline on a newspaper front page story, or on a press advertisement.

If you are in a round-table discussion, and want to make an intervention that gets attention, you could take your cue from what someone else says, adding an intriguing twist, then pausing while everyone focuses attention on you. The pause is an important part of the process. It lends weight to your opening statement or question, and gives you control. Don't rush to speak.

One word of caution: once you have their attention you must not change the subject. Expand on what you have just said, then lead them to your structured message.

Keep 'em

Remember the sequence of persuasion: attention – interest – desire – action.

Once you have caught the attention of your listener(s), you must keep on track with some benefit or item that serves their self-interest. A potent formula is a mixture of benefits and how-it-works. For your proposition to succeed, your pile of benefits must outweigh the cost or pain of making the change.

For your audience to stay with you, there must be a clear build-up of benefits. If you are addressing an audience in a formal way, you will have more time. The audience will expect you to take your allotted time span to develop your case.

In informal situations the rules are different. As soon as you have grabbed their attention with your hook (and paused for it to make its full impact), you need to deliver a summary of your case. In such situations (usually called 'meetings') you should anticipate that the other participants are not terribly interested in hearing what you have to say, and will interrupt with their own ideas as soon as you pause for breath ... unless you give a brief outline and ask for their agreement that you should flesh it out.

That first phase (hook plus outline) should take no more than two to three minutes to tell. One minute is best. If they are hooked and consent to a fuller account, you are on firmer ground and can take your time.

Konvince 'em

Persuasion is the process of getting others to act differently. However, it must be preceded by some change in their thinking. They need to be convinced.

What convinces people most effectively? Evidence.

Whatever claims you make, be sure to back it up with evidence.

Kore message

This is the take-away idea mentioned in Chapter 10, as the M in OH AM I SAD.

It's the central idea that you want people to understand, carry away and remember. It's the primary purpose of your speech. If you are making a one-minute speech, it could be the entire speech.

How to make a one-minute speech

The key elements are:
◆ establish context or commonality
◆ hook
◆ theme
◆ need or problem
◆ benefit / disadvantage
◆ offer solution / make a proposition
◆ outcome.

Mental preparation

Remember that you can say a lot in 60 seconds, but not *about* a lot. It's not enough time to make more than one point, unless you intend it merely to 'trail' a longer speech or presentation, in which case you would use the time to outline the menu, agenda or list of contents.

For the most part, however, you should think of making a single point, and making it well. Before you speak, be clear about the point you want to make. Do not try to make a comprehensive statement about your theme, but rather ask yourself: 'What can I tell them that they will not hear from someone else?'. Or, 'What do I really want to tell them?'.

Start by sending out a carrier wave, some way of **establishing common ground**, e.g. 'We are all communicators here ...' or 'It's the question we speakers are always asking ourselves ...'

Quickly move to your **hook**. In fact, you could use the hook to establish common ground, combining the first two stages, e.g. 'This year Americans will pay over 38 billion dollars to hear someone speak. I'll translate that into English. They'll pay 24 billion pounds to hear someone speak ...'

Then state your **theme**, e.g 'I'd like to tell you what you need to become a professional speaker.'

State the **main benefit**, e.g. 'With the right guidance you could qualify for the high fees that top professional speakers are paid.'

Mention a **possible obstacle**, e.g. 'It's not as easy as you might think, and if you get it wrong it could take a long time to claw your way back.'

Then make a **proposition**, e.g. 'You need to set aside at least one half day, and preferably two, to learn the secrets of becoming a professional speaker.'

Finally, focus on an **outcome**, e.g. 'If you are serious about a career as a speaker, register now for my seminar, Be Paid To Speak.'

This is, of course, just an example. In the next chapter you will find a number of examples of short messages: elevator speeches, radio commercials, soundbites, poetry, and extracts from speeches. The common factors are (a) the single point that each makes and (b) the brevity with which the point is made.

In summary ...

- ◆ Have something to say.
- ◆ Really want to say it.
- ◆ Develop the right technique for putting it across.
- ◆ You've got to 'Katch 'em' first.
- ◆ ... then 'Keep 'em'.
- ◆ ... then 'Konvince 'em'.
- ◆ ... focusing on your 'Kore Message'.
- ◆ Finally, learn to construct a 60-second speech.

Chapter 12

Examples of 60-second Messages

In this Chapter:

◆ **elevator speeches**

◆ **radio commercials**

◆ **soundbites**

◆ **poetry**

◆ **extracts from speeches.**

Concise messages need not all be 60-seconds long. They should be no longer than that, but could be as short as 12 seconds. The examples in this chapter say what needs to be said in about 60 seconds or less.

Elevator speeches

Typically, you have 12-16 seconds to tell someone what you do, in such a way as to persuade them to say, 'Tell me more.'

Plumbing services
'You know how the central heating or plumbing always seems to break down at weekends, which means that you have to make endless phone calls or pay over the odds to get someone to fix it?

Well, I provide a service that takes care of all that for you, which means that you only make a single call to us and we get someone to fix the problem fast, and at a reasonable cost.'

Telecommunications consultant

'You know how, when you call the telephone company or any other service, you have to go through an endless menu of selections without speaking to a human being, so that you end up frustrated and angry? Well, what I do is to advise such companies on a better way to handle calls, so that they improve relationships with their customers instead of alienating them.'

Customer service

'You know how shop assistants these days seem less and less interested in serving their customers, so that you sometimes walk out without buying? Well, when that happens, the company is losing sales and goodwill. So, what I do is to train shop staff to adopt a more helpful attitude and improve their selling skills, so that the customers gain and the company gains.'

Radio commercials

The most common length of a commercial is 30 seconds, although some are a little longer. It is rare for one to be more than 60 seconds. This is because of the attention span of the listener, especially for a sales message. It is therefore especially important to use drama or some other active ingredient to lift the message above the level of the ordinary, and to distinguish it from the programme it interrupts.

For a charity for the blind

'Imagine feeling the wind in your face and raindrops falling on your head, and not knowing if it was night or day.

Imagine hearing sudden laughter and not knowing if they were laughing at you.

Imagine smiling at someone you'd just met and not knowing if he or she was smiling back.

Imagine waiting for a bus and not being able to tell if it was coming along.

Imagine never being able to watch television or see another movie ever again.

Imagine what it means to have the gift of sight.

Imagine being able to give that gift to someone else.

All it takes is a gift of £XX to pay for a cataract operation.'

For a charity for the deaf

'This is a special announcement for those who can hear. Now here's a special announcement for those who cannot hear.

[5 seconds' silence]

That was a small sample of what a deaf person hears all day and all night.

Total silence.

It's not easy to cope with our noisy world when you cannot hear a thing. No radio. No telephones. No mobile phones to say you're on the train. No conversations unless you can see people's faces.

The RNID exists to help the deaf to cope as well as the rest of us. The RNID needs your help. Will you help?'

Soundbites

Report on survey

'According to a National Survey of Hospitals, the Branchester Hospital is the tenth best hospital in the country, although it is little known outside its catchment area. The survey covered such essential matters as staffing, waiting times, facilities and patient confidence, and what was particularly significant was its mortality index. The index reveals a hospital's death rate against a national average of 100, and Branchester Hospital's score was 95, which is five points better than the national average.'

President Clinton on Monica Lewinsky

'I tried to walk a fine line between acting lawfully and testifying falsely, but I now recognise that I did not fully accomplish that goal, and that certain of my responses to questions about Ms Lewinsky were false. I hope my actions today will help to bring closure and finality to these matters.'

Telephone contact

Referral call

'Good morning. My name is John Smith. I believe we have a mutual friend – Bill Brown – and Bill very kindly gave me your name because I was talking to him about an interesting approach to PR. He thought you might be interested to hear about it as well, because you might be planning a PR campaign. Is that right? (pause for reply) Is this a convenient time to talk about it, or would you prefer me to call you later/tomorrow?'

Cold call

'Good morning. My name is John Smith of Pensions Unlimited. I realise that you have probably had more than enough calls from financial advisers, but I'm calling you in case you have not yet done anything about the government's latest ruling on deferred pensions. If you could let me have a few minutes of your time, either now or later today, I can promise that you will find it of interest. Is it convenient to speak now, or would you prefer me to call back at 2:30 this afternoon ?'

From famous poets

Mark Antony on Brutus (Shakespeare)

This was the noblest Roman of them all:
All the conspirators save only he
Did what they did in envy of great Caesar;
He only, in a general honest thought,
And common good to all, made one of them.
His life was gentle, and the elements
So mix'd in him that Nature might stand up
And say to all the world, 'This was a man!'

Leisure (W H Davies)

What is this life if, full of care,
We have no time to stand and stare?
No time to stand beneath the boughs
And stare as long as sheep and cows.
No time to see, when woods we pass,
Where squirrels hide their nuts in grass.
No time to see, in broad daylight,
Streams full of stars, like skies at night.
No time to turn at Beauty's glance

And watch her feet, how they can dance.
No time to wait till her mouth can
Enrich that smile her eyes began.
A poor life this if, full of care,
We have no time to stand and stare.

Extracts from speeches

Do it now

'Develop the habit of doing it now. Recognise that whatever you do today must be important, because it will cost a day of your life to achieve it. Don't waste today – it's a slice of your life that you can never retrieve.'

As Stephen Grellett so memorably put it, "I expect to pass through this world but once, and I shall not pass this way again."

'We are not prisoners of the past. And we need not wait for tomorrow. We are here today. The task is before us today. Let us therefore seize the day, DO IT NOW, and discover the scope of our skills – today! Tomorrow just will not do.'

Courage

'Courage is the power of the spirit. Napoleon said that power is either of the sword or of the spirit, and ultimately it's the power of the spirit that will triumph. It's what gives us our values of truth, honesty and integrity. It's what separates the best from the rest, the noble from the feeble, the leader from the pack. You know you have courage when your mind says 'Quit!' but your spirit won't let you.'